JOSEF MENGELE

JOSEF MENGELE

Other books in the Heroes and Villains series include:

JOSEF MENGELE

John F. Grabowski

LUCENT BOOKS®

THOMSON
GALE

San Diego • Detroit • New York • San Francisco • Cleveland • New Haven, Conn. • Waterville, Maine • London • Munich

THOMSON

——✦——™

GALE

On cover: Josef Mengele, the Nazi doctor known as the Angel of Death, stands at a train window in his SS uniform.

For more information, contact
Lucent Books
27500 Drake Rd.
Farmington Hills, MI 48331-3535
Or you can visit our Internet site at http://www.gale.com

LIBRARY OF CONGRESS CATALOGING-IN-PUBLICATION DATA

Grabowski, John F.
    Josef Mengele / by John F. Grabowski
p. cm. — (Heroes and villains)
Summary: Profiles the Nazi war criminal who was personally responsible for deciding which inmates of the concentration camp at Auschwitz would work, which would be subjected to experimentation, and which would die.
Includes bibliographical references.
    ISBN 1-59018-425-4 (hardback : alk. paper)
    1. Mengele, Josef, 1911—Juvenile literature. 2. War criminals—Germany—Biography—Juvenile literature. 3. World War, 1939–1945—Atrocities—Juvenile literature. 4. Germany—Social conditions—1933–1945—Juvenile literature. 5. Physicians—Germany—Biography—Juvenile literature. [1. Mengele, Josef, 1911– 2. War criminals—Germany. 3. World War, 1939–1945—Atrocities. 4. Germany—Social conditions—1933–1945. 5. Physicians.] I. Title. II. Heroes and villains series.
    DD247.M46G73 2004
    940.534'18'092—dc21

                                                                2003011132

Printed in the United States of America

Contents

Foreword

Good and evil are an ever-present feature of human history. Their presence is reflected through the ages in tales of great heroism and extraordinary villainy. Such tales provide insight into human nature, whether they involve two people or two thousand, for the essence of heroism and villainy is found in deeds rather than in numbers. It is the deeds that pique our interest and lead us to wonder what prompts a man or woman to perform such acts.

Samuel Johnson, the eminent eighteenth-century English writer, once wrote, "The two great movers of the human mind are the desire for good, and fear of evil." The pairing of desire and fear, possibly two of the strongest human emotions, helps explain the intense fascination people have with all things good and evil—and by extension, heroic and villainous.

People are attracted to the person who reaches into a raging river to pull a child from what could have been a watery grave for both, and to the person who risks his or her own life to shepherd hundreds of desperate black slaves to safety on the Underground Railroad. We wonder what qualities these heroes possess that enable them to act against self-interest, and even their own survival. We also wonder if, under similar circumstances, we would behave as they do.

Evil, on the other hand, horrifies as well as intrigues us. Few people can look upon the drifter who mutilates and kills a neighbor or the dictator who presides over the torture and murder of thousands of his own citizens without feeling a sense of revulsion. And yet, as Joseph Conrad writes, we experience "the fascination of the abomination." How else to explain the overwhelming success of a book such as Truman Capote's *In Cold Blood*, which examines in horrifying detail a vicious and senseless murder that took place in the American heartland in the 1960s? The popularity of murder mysteries and Court TV are also evidence of the human fascination with villainy.

Most people recoil in the face of such evil. Yet most feel a deep-seated curiosity about the kind of person who could commit a terrible act. It is perhaps a reflection of our innermost fears that we wonder whether we could resist or stand up to such behavior in our presence or even if we ourselves possess the capacity to commit such terrible crimes.

The Lucent Books Heroes and Villains series capitalizes on our fascination with the perpetrators of both good and evil by introducing readers to some of history's most revered heroes and hated villains. These include heroes such as Frederick Douglass, who knew firsthand the humiliation of slavery and, at great risk to himself, publicly fought to abolish the institution of slavery in America. It also includes villains such as Adolf Hitler, who is remembered both for the devastation of Europe and for the murder of 6 million Jews and thousands of Gypsies, Slavs, and others whom Hitler deemed unworthy of life.

Each book in the Heroes and Villains series examines the life story of a hero or villain from history. Generous use of primary and secondary source quotations gives readers eyewitness views of the life and times of each individual as well as enlivens the narrative. Notes and annotated bibliographies provide stepping-stones to further research.

The Personification of Evil

The story of Josef Mengele has been embellished by the faulty memories, unconfirmed rumors, and disputed accounts of those with whom he came into contact over the years. Enough evidence remains, however, to warrant his reputation as one of history's most feared and hated cold-blooded mass murderers, a man responsible for the deaths of some four hundred thousand people.

A Matter of Life and Death

For thousands of Jews transported to the concentration camps at Auschwitz during World War II, Mengele was the person responsible for deciding who would be sent to death in the gas chambers, who would be used for slave labor, and who would become subjects for his ghastly experiments designed to uncover the secrets of human genetics.

He personally sent between two hundred thousand and four hundred thousand inmates to their deaths, his hatred for Jews the main impetus for doing the unimaginable. "They come here as Jews," he is reported to have said, "and leave as smoke up a chimney."[1]

How did a scientist and doctor—someone dedicated to improving the lot of mankind—descend into the depths, as did Mengele? A question perhaps even harder to answer is how a person could commit such atrocities and never show the least bit of regret for his actions. Even years later, in a letter to his son, Rolf, Mengele wrote, "I can never hope that you will understand or sympathize with the course of my life. But I have not the slightest reason to justify, or apologize for, any of my decisions or actions."[2]

Escaping the Net

Approximately 150,000 Nazis were identified as war criminals for committing crimes against humanity during World War II. Of those, about 40,000 were formally charged and 10,000 eventually convicted. Of those who escaped, Josef Mengele became the top target for Nazi hunters around the world. As time went by, he achieved a mythic status for his ability to evade his pursuers. His notoriety grew with the release of two popular novels and movies of the 1970s,

Josef Mengele is one of history's cold-blooded mass murderers.

William Goldman's *Marathon Man* and Ira Levin's *The Boys from Brazil*, in which Mengele's character was the central villain.

It is not surprising, therefore, that so many voices from around the world called for the capture of the man whose unspeakable experiments at Auschwitz shocked humanity. As famed Nazi-hunter Simon Wiesenthal said of Mengele several years ago, "He is a very important witness at a time when we have denials of the Holocaust and denials of the gas chambers. What we're doing is a warning for the murderers of tomorrow. Even forty years later, 10,000 miles from the crime—you cannot escape justice."[3]

Unfortunately, despite the efforts of national governments, intelligence agencies, and private individuals around the globe, Mengele did in fact escape. To those for whom he embodied a dark past they hoped to exorcise, the discovery of his death in 1985 brought what Rabbi Marvin Hier of the Simon Wiesenthal Center in Los Angeles called, "a sad sense of relief."[4] Though the forty-year hunt for Mengele had finally come to an end, it was an unsatisfying conclusion. Many still wished to understand the mystery of how a highly educated person from a well-to-do family, trained in the sciences and medicine, could be transformed into an insensitive monster capable of perpetrating the most horrible atrocities imaginable on his fellow human beings.

Chapter One

GROWING UP IN GÜNZBURG

The tiny village of Günzburg, Bavaria, is located about halfway between Munich and Stuttgart in southwest Germany on the banks of the Günz River, which eventually flows into the mighty Danube. The little town lies amid the fertile farmland of the Bavarian district known as Swabia. The picturesque hamlet was the birthplace and childhood home of the man remembered today as the infamous Angel of Death.

The Mengeles of Günzburg

Josef Mengele was born on March 16, 1911. Named for his maternal grandfather, he was the firstborn son of Karl and Walburga Mengele. (Three years earlier his mother had given birth to a stillborn child.) The couple would have two other sons, Karl Jr., born in 1912,

and Alois (known as Lolo), born two years later.

Josef's ancestors were also from the region around Günzburg. Alois, his paternal grandfather, came from the village of Lutzingen. He married Theresia Mayr, a native of nearby Hochstadt, and ran a business manufacturing bricks. Alois was successful enough to enable him to send his son Karl—Josef's father—to school to obtain a university degree.

The Family Business

Karl Sr. settled in Günzburg as a young man. It was there, while studying to become an engineer, that he met and married Walburga Hupfauer, who was four years younger than he. The couple moved into a small house that they shared with another family.

In 1907 Karl became a partner in a foundry that manufactured farm equipment. He was loaned the money needed to start the business by Walburga's parents, who were wealthy farmers. Karl's partner was a mechanic named Andreas Eisenlauer. The very same year that Karl bought into the business, the foundry was destroyed by a fire. Using the money he received from the insurance company, Karl bought a piece of land and rebuilt the concern. Two years later, Eisenlauer pulled out of the partnership due to poor health. Under Karl's management, the seven-employee company, now bearing his name, prospered. He was a stern but fair employer who put his engineering talents to work by designing new machines that cut down on the time needed for farm chores such as cutting chaff and spreading manure. He reportedly received patents for several of his inventions.

A Dominating Female Presence

When World War I broke out, Karl entered the military and served as an infantryman on the western front.

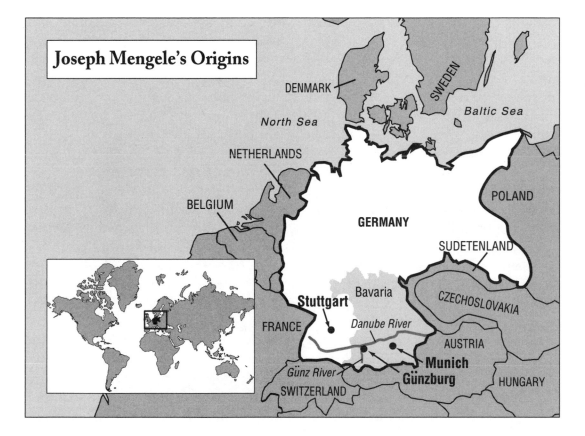

Joseph Mengele's Origins

DENMARK

SWEDEN

North Sea

Baltic Sea

NETHERLANDS

BELGIUM

POLAND

GERMANY

SUDETENLAND

CZECHOSLOVAKIA

Stuttgart

Bavaria

FRANCE

Danube River

AUSTRIA

Günz River

Munich

Günzburg

SWITZERLAND

HUNGARY

Karl Mengele & Sons

The company founded by Karl Mengele in 1907 eventually became the largest employer in Günzburg. The huge farm machinery factory dominated the village for the better part of the twentieth century, engaging as many as one thousand employees. The tractors produced by the firm were sold from Australia to South America. Even association with the mass killing of millions of Jews could not tarnish the distinctive Mengele brand name.

Alois Mengele and his brother, Karl Jr., took over the business after their father's death. When Alois died in the mid-seventies, control of the firm passed on to Josef Mengele's nephews, Karl Heinz and Dieter Mengele. The nephews eventually sold it in 1996. Today, the factory buildings serve as a supermarket.

Walburga took over the management of the company. A fierce disciplinarian, she drove the workers as hard as—if not harder than—her husband, and the business continued to grow. It was while under her command that the company won a contract to produce a special army vehicle—called the *Fouragewagen*—for the kaiser (head of the German government).

The massive Walburga suffered from weight problems all her life. She was a compulsive eater who eventually became so obese she could barely walk. When she visited the factory, dressed all in black, she presented a fearsome facade. Frightened by her fierce temper, the workers stayed out of her way as much as possible, calling her "the Matador" behind her back.

Even Karl failed to escape Walburga's wrath. Shortly after Josef's birth, the company had become successful enough for Karl to afford to buy his first new car. Upon seeing it for the first time, Walburga began screaming uncontrollably, furious that her husband had made such an expensive purchase without first consulting with her.

A Disciplined Upbringing

Karl and Walburga demanded the same respect and obedience from their sons as they did from their employees. Although displays of love and affection were rare in the household, Josef nonetheless was remembered as a happy child. Neighbors recalled him playing in the fields in the area with his brother, going on family outings with his parents, and attending skating parties on a small pond near their home.

Nicknamed Beppo, Josef was frail and often fell victim to sickness and accidents. (When he was six years old, he nearly drowned when he fell into a barrel holding rainwater.) His fragility led to his isolation from others his age but caused him to receive extra attention from his mother, whom he both liked and admired.

Mengele remembered his mother as "very strict; she treated us severely. She was a woman of strong character."[5] He still preferred her company and occasional rages, however, to that of his father, whose life revolved around his business. As a child, Josef did not see much of his father, since Karl spent a good deal of time traveling from farm to farm in an effort to sell his products. (Josef did have a great deal of admiration for Karl Sr. for having made a success of himself through his own efforts.) It is conceivable that Walburga's cold-hearted demeanor may have been a contributing factor to the indifference to life shown by her son in future years.

Walburga was a devout Catholic who insisted that her sons strictly practice the faith. Her values were upheld by a woman named Monika, who was the boys' nanny when they were young. As they got older, however, the strictness of their upbringing eventually turned Josef away from the church.

A Dependable Youngster

As the Mengele's oldest son, Josef had his hand in the family business at an early age. When he was nine, he would take the family's horse-drawn wagon to the railroad station to meet the trains bringing supplies to his father's factory. He would order his two younger brothers to help with the unloading of the parcels from the train. Josef then supervised as the packages were packed onto the wagon, making sure nothing was broken or left behind. He then brought the wagon back home, guiding the horses through Günzburg's cobblestone streets.

Josef was proud of the fact that he was given so much responsibility by his father. He carried out his chores with diligence in an effort to show his parents that he was dependable and worthy of their trust. This devotion carried over to his schoolwork.

A Bright Student

Despite the Mengele family's wealth and ability to afford private schooling, Josef attended a public elementary school. There he proved to be a bright, ambitious student—though never the smartest in his class—who developed a strong interest in art and music. The well-behaved youngster continuously earned praise from his teachers for his conduct, punctuality, and responsibility.

By the time Josef was eleven years old, his family was wealthy enough to afford a home of their own. They moved into a villa across the street from the gymnasium, or high school, that he would attend. There Josef's progress was again interrupted by illness. When he was fifteen, he missed more than half a year of school when he was diagnosed with osteomylitis, an inflammation of the bone marrow. He also suffered from nephritis, a painful inflammation of the kidneys. Once again bedridden, he was deprived of needed social contact.

When Josef returned to his studies, his interests turned to the sciences. He was determined to do better than his two brothers, particularly Karl Jr., of whom he was very jealous. Josef's favorite subjects became biology, zoology, physics, and especially anthropology. Given the drive to succeed that had been instilled in him by his parents, Josef had great plans for the future. As former schoolmate Julius Diesbach recalled, "Josef was a very ambitious young man with a great need to succeed. . . . He once told me that one day I would read his name in the encyclopedia."[6]

A Developing Social Life

Outside of school Josef began to develop his social skills. He dressed immaculately, wearing expensive suits and carrying a pair of white gloves whenever he went out on the town with his friends. He became an excellent ballroom dancer, which taken together with his dark, Mediterranean good looks made him a favorite with the young ladies of Günzburg.

Josef had a taste for the finer things in life. He was more interested in fast, expensive cars, dances, swimming par-

ties, and going to the opera than in politics. Together with many of his friends, however, he did join the *Grossdeutscher Jugendbund*, or Greater Germany Youth Movement. According to authors Lucette Matalon Lagnado and Sheila Cohn Dekel, "The upper-middle-class German youth of that era volunteered for the *Grossdeutscher Jugendbund* almost as reflexively as their American counterparts were signing up for the Boy Scouts."[7]

The patriotic group was associated with the German Soldiers' League, popularly known as the *Stahlhelm*, or Steel Helmets. The *Stahlhelm* was a nationalistic paramilitary organization with deep-rooted interests in seeing Germany return to its days of pre–World War I glory. Under the terms of the 1919 Treaty of Versailles, which ended World War I, Germany was forced, among other things, to accept all blame for the war, to pay reparations to the Allies, to reduce its army to one hundred thousand men, to destroy its air force, and to give up all of its colonies. Such terms were humiliating to the proud German people. The *Stahlhelm's* ideals appealed to both Josef and his friends. As the group's 1928 resolution proclaimed,

We hate the present form of the German state with all our hearts because it denies to us the hope of freeing our enslaved fatherland. It denies us any opportunity to

Boys of the Greater Germany Youth Movement march in a parade. Mengele joined the movement as a teenager.

Stahlhelm

The *Stahlhelm* that Mengele joined as a young man was a nationalistic paramilitary organization whose members wore the steel helmets from which the group derived its name. Aside from the swastika, the steel helmet is arguably the most recognizable symbol of the Third Reich.

The *Stahlhelm* was a direct descendant of the German light medieval helmet (sallet) of the fifteenth century. It was revived during World War I and, with slight variations, stayed in production through 1945. Initially painted gray-green, the version worn by the *Wehrmacht* was repainted dark gray after spring 1940. At the beginning of World War II, it was worn with a silver-gray eagle decal on the left and a tricolor shield of black, white, and red on the right. The decals were ordered painted over in 1940 since they made convenient aiming points for snipers. The SS wore the same color helmet as the *Wehrmacht*, but with different decals.

Soldiers in the *Stahlhelm* stand at attention. The group's name was derived from their steel helmets.

cleanse the German people from the war-guilt lie and works against the grain of necessary living space in Eastern Europe.[8]

This desire to return Germany to its former glory would become a driving force over the course of his life.

Josef passed his *Abitur*, or preliminary college entry exam, in April 1930. His father wanted his oldest son to follow him into the family business—possibly as an accountant—but Josef had other ideas. More interested in research and discovery, he considered becoming a dentist but finally decided to concentrate on medicine, with a special emphasis on anthropology and genetics. He decided to leave the shadow of the family business in Günzburg to strike out on his own, away from the control of his domineering mother and hard-driving father. That fall the handsome nineteen-year-old left home and traveled east to enroll at Munich University in the Bavarian capital city.

A Center of Political Turmoil
Munich in 1930 was a center of political unrest. Many Germans felt that through the Treaty of Versailles, their country had been made a scapegoat by the other nations. This anger incited a great deal of chaos over the ensuing years and led to the formation of several extremist political parties. One of these was the German Workers' Party, later to become the National Socialist German Workers' Party (NSDAP), or Nazi Party.

The Weimar Republic, Germany's ruling government, could not control the various factions, whose anger was further inflamed by the inflation, unemployment, and economic upheaval that wracked the country. By 1930 Adolf Hitler had taken over control of the NSDAP, winning converts to his cause with his overly patriotic ideas and racist theories that blamed the Jews for all of Germany's problems.

Hitler's movement was centered in Munich, where his inflammatory speeches denounced the Jews as being a race that was less than human. His dream of a new, powerful Aryan empire, populated by a German super-race, was met with approval by the crowds who heard his hate-filled words and call for racial purity. By 1931 the NSDAP had become the second-largest party in the German parliament.

Social Darwinist Theory
Until his arrival in Munich, Mengele had not shown much interest in political affairs. He was fascinated by the energetic, sophisticated city with its fine restaurants, stylish stores and shops, and myriad cultural outlets. Like many students of the day, however, he grew more and more receptive to Hitler's nationalistic ravings and dreams of a new Germany that would once again become a world power. As he wrote in his unpublished biography, "I was strongly

The Aryans

The word "Aryan" is derived from the Sanskrit word *arya*, meaning "noble." According to author Leni Yahil, it was originally used by linguists to refer to the group of languages from which the modern Indo-Germanic languages are descended. The people who spoke these languages—Aryans—are believed to have settled around Iran and northern India in prehistoric times.

Because of their structure, vocabulary, and complexity, these languages are considered by eighteenth-century linguists to be superior to the Semitic tongues of the Near East. This led some people to the conclusion that the people who spoke them were

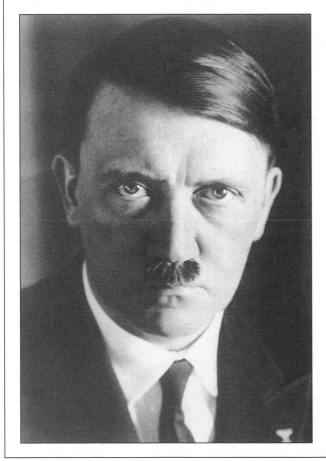

themselves superior. Nationalistic German scholars chose to believe that these people were a tall, blond, Nordic race originally from Europe near the Baltic Sea.

One of the major proponents of the theory of Aryan supremacy was Joseph-Arthur, comte de (count of) Gobineau. In his most influential work, the four-volume, mid-1850s *Essai sur l'inégalité des races humaines* (Essay on the Inequality of Human Races), de Gobineau declared the superiority of the white race over others. He argued that the white race would prosper only if it did not become contaminated by mixing with other races. This belief eventually became one of the major principles of Nazi philosophy.

Adolf Hitler is history's foremost proponent of Aryan supremacy.

attracted by the program and the whole organization of the National Socialists."[9]

Hitler's ideas, in part, were derived from the theories of the social Darwinists of the late nineteenth century. The Darwinists believed that all problems—both social and physical—were inherited from previous generations. If those individuals who exhibited "negative" characteristics were prevented from having children, and those genetically fit encouraged to have more, only the more desired traits would be passed on. As a result the entire race would improve over time.

Scientists and nations around the globe began to accept Darwinist theories. People looked to the new field of eugenics (which comes from the Greek word for "good genes") as a way of working for a better world. In Germany, however, Hitler's application of these principles took on a decidedly anti-Semitic slant. His plan for a race of supermen and superwomen depended on the elimination of the Jews—among others—whom he considered inferior.

Inspired by Hitler's oratory, Mengele formally enlisted in the *Stahlhelm* in May 1931 at the age of twenty. His love for his homeland made it easy for him to accept Hitler's assertions that placed the blame for all of Germany's woes on the Jews and other non-Aryans. Although he would not join the Nazi Party for another six years, his father had already made a commitment to them. Karl Sr. had been friends with Georg Deisenhofer,

English naturalist Charles Darwin. Hitler's plan to create a superior race was based in part on Darwin's theory of evolution.

the regional party chief, for some time. In 1932 Hitler visited Günzburg and gave a speech at the Mengele factory. After Hitler came into power as Germany's dictator, Deisenhofer rewarded Karl Sr. for his party loyalty with a seat on the Günzburg town council. His connections with the Nazis paid off. Mengele's business increased, and by 1936 he had three hundred fifty people working for him.

In the meantime Josef had become even more serious about his studies. He decided that his real interest lay in evolution rather than in medicine. Mengele took to his work with renewed vigor and ambition. He was determined to make a success of himself in his chosen field and to work for the betterment of his beloved homeland.

Rüdin's Influence

At the university Mengele regularly attended lectures given by Dr. Ernst Rüdin. Rüdin was one of the leading proponents of a theory that called for the extermination of people he deemed inferior. He believed that the lives of those afflicted with particular disabilities served no purpose and should be eliminated for the betterment of the race. He went so far as to suggest that doctors had a responsibility to destroy such life. Mengele's acceptance of this philosophy would help explain his ability in future years to experiment on concentration camp inmates without showing the slightest bit of remorse.

In 1933, shortly after the NSDAP came into power, Rüdin was instrumental in helping to write Hitler's Law for the Protection of Hereditary Health. The law established the mental and physical criteria under which sterilization could be imposed on someone "if, in the judgment of medical science, it could be expected that his descendants will suffer from serious inherited mental or physical defects."[10] The law affected those who suffered from congenital feeblemindedness, schizophrenia, manic-depression, congenital epilepsy, inheritable St. Vitus dance (Huntington's chorea), hereditary blindness, hereditary deafness, serious inheritable malformations, and chronic alcoholism. This law preventing such people from reproducing marked only the beginning of a series of programs aimed at purifying German stock by ridding it of those deemed undesirable or biologically inferior. These programs would ultimately culminate in Hitler's *Die Endlösung*, or Final Solution—the plan to exterminate Jews from the European continent.

Earning His Degree

In January 1934 Hitler ordered the *Sturmabteilung* (German for "Assault Division," sometimes referred to as storm troopers) to absorb the *Stahlhelm*. The *Sturmabteilung*, or Brownshirts, functioned as body guards to enforce order at Nazi meetings and gatherings. Mengele remained with them until October 1934, when he left because of

Nazi storm troopers march in formation during a rally. Mengele joined the Nazi Party in 1937.

a kidney ailment. He turned all of his time and attention to his studies as he continued on in quest of his degree.

Another person who had a significant effect on Mengele's development at Munich University was Professor T. Mollinson. Mollinson believed it was

possible to identify someone of Jewish extraction by physical characteristics alone. Following in his footsteps, Mengele wrote his Ph.D. dissertation on "Racial Morphological Research on the Lower Jaw Section of Four Racial Groups." In 1935 he was awarded his doctorate in philosophy for the work, which concluded that one could differentiate between four specific racial groups (Egyptians, Melanesians, short-skulled Europeans, and long-skulled Europeans) solely by the structure of the lower jaw (a scientifically unsound conclusion).

The following summer Mengele passed his state medical examination. He took a job as a resident junior doctor in Leipzig at the university medical clinic. While there he met Irene Schoenbein, the daughter of one of the university's professors. Irene was a well-educated young woman who had attended school in Switzerland and Italy, where she studied art history. She loved to travel and read and spoke four languages. Mengele began courting the attractive nineteen-year-old blonde, whom he called "the great love of my life."[11]

Chapter Two

DOCTOR MENGELE

In looking toward his future, possibly with Irene, it did not take Mengele long to realize that he was more interested in his genetic research and a career in academics than in medicine. He remained at the clinic for four months before taking on a new position that would mark a turning point in his career.

The trail that eventually led Josef Mengele to the concentration camps at Auschwitz began in the smoky beer halls of Munich. There Adolph Hitler spouted his anti-Semitic ravings to German citizens looking for someone to lead them out of the economic morass that was post-World War I Germany. Hitler directed their anger and hostility toward the Jews. For Mengele that animosity was engendered at the University of Frankfurt. It

was there that he met Otmar Freiherr von Verschuer, who would play a most significant role in determining the direction of his life.

Otmar Freiherr von Verschuer

By 1935 anti-Semitism and the concept of racial purity had become firmly entrenched in all walks of German life. Jews were labeled money-hungry leeches who were trying to drive the country to ruin. In school Mengele was taught the writings of political philosophers like Paul Anton de Lagarde, who openly expressed his hatred for

> those who out of humanity defend these Jews, or who are too cowardly to trample these usurious vermin to death. . . . With trichinae and bacilli one does not negotiate, nor

are trichinae and bacilli to be educated. They are exterminated as quickly and thoroughly as possible.[12]

In his widely read volume, *Mein Kampf*, Hitler had even placed his hatred of the Jews in a religious context.

"I believe that I am acting in accordance with the will of the Almighty Creator," he wrote. "By defending myself against the Jew, I am fighting for the work of the Lord."[13] In September 1935 he began formalizing the government's policies toward the Jews with the announcement of two measures that

Nazi soldiers and civilians gather around a poster which proclaims, "The Jews are our misfortune." Such anti-Semitic propaganda was common throughout Nazi Germany.

came to be known as the Nuremberg Laws. The Law for the Protection of German Blood and German Honor prohibited marriages and sexual relations between Jews and "citizens of German or kindred blood,"[14] and prohibited Jews from hiring Germans as servants. The Reich Citizenship Law stripped Jews of their German citizenship and effectively expelled them from all professions.

The Nuremberg Laws were implemented by the top scientists at the leading research centers in Germany. One of those most active in this area was Professor Otmar Freiherr von Verschuer of the University of Frankfurt, arguably the most renowned racial scientist of the day. Von Verschuer, who praised Hitler for being the first statesman "to recognize hereditary biological and race hygiene,"[15] helped establish the Institute for Heredity, Biology, and Racial Purity at the University of Frankfurt.

The Institute for Heredity, Biology, and Racial Purity

On January 1, 1937, after having received a recommendation from Professor Mollinson, Mengele applied for—and received—a position as a research assistant at the institute. He joined von Verschuer's staff at what was the center of Nazi philosophical and scientific thinking. Mengele soon became von Verschuer's favorite student. Far from his home in Günzburg

he was a frequent guest at the professor's residence. By applying himself to his work, he earned his mentor's praise—the affirmation and approval that had been missing from his childhood when his father had shown more interest in his business than in his family. Von Verschuer became a father figure to Mengele, someone he did his utmost to please.

During this period of time the ministry of health in Frankfurt established a special unit whose job it was to determine the purity of the Aryan ancestry of the city's residents. As von Verschuer's assistant, one of Mengele's responsibilities at the institute was to aid in this evaluation. His reports were used in judicial investigations that involved violations of the Nuremberg Laws. In future years they would also be helpful when the Nazis were rooting out all those of Jewish ancestry for deportation to the concentration camps.

It was through von Verschuer that Mengele became intrigued by the role that twins could play in genetic research. A decade earlier von Verschuer's work as head of the genetics department at the Kaiser Wilhelm Institute in Berlin led him to the conclusion that by studying twins, he could better understand the laws of genetics. His work was based solely on observations, however, since the laws of the day forbade him from using human beings as experimental guinea pigs.

The Lebensborn

One of the most horrifying programs instituted by the Nazis was the Lebensborn ("spring of life") project. Created by Heinrich Himmler in December 1935, the *Lebensborn Eingetragener Verein* (Registered Society Lebensborn) was an organization that attempted to encourage young, "racially pure" girls to give birth to children who would then be raised as part of the super race. The Lebensborn centers, as such, were originally nurseries for these children.

By 1939, however, a second component of the program had been put into effect. Thousands of children who matched the ideal Nazi racial criteria (such as blond hair and blue eyes) were kidnapped from the eastern occupied countries by the SS. They were transported to Lebensborn centers where they were "Germanized." The children were often persuaded that they had been abandoned by their parents, and indoctrinated into the Nazi system.

It is estimated that more than a quarter of a million children were kidnapped and sent back to Germany in this way. Some eventually were adopted by SS families, but thousands were sent to concentration camps where they were killed. Following the end of World War II, approximately twenty-five thousand of these children were returned to their families.

The New Nazi

By May 1937 Mengele was completely committed to Nazi ideals and philosophy. He applied for membership in the party, was accepted, and was issued membership number 5574974. He also applied for membership in the SS (*Schutzstaffel*, or defense squadron, that began as Hitler's personal guard unit). After a thorough examination of his background—which was found to be free of Jewish blood over the previous four generations—he was accepted in May 1938.

As a matter of course all new SS members were required to have their blood type tattooed on their skin in case it became necessary to give them a transfusion. Because of his vanity Mengele did not want to be tattooed. He was able to avoid this by convincing the SS that the procedure was unnecessary. Any competent physician would check a patient's blood type himself before performing surgery, he maintained, rather than relying on a tattoo. He did not know it at the time, but doing this would help him avoid capture by the Allied forces when the war ended.

In July 1938 Mengele was awarded his medical degree by Frankfurt University. His professional career was beginning to bring him success and recognition. That same year he had his second doctoral dissertation published, this one entitled "Genealogical Studies in the Cases of Cleft Lip-Jaw-Palate." Whereas his first paper had been primarily based on facts, this new work began to allude to ideas that were not based on science, mainly that there was a racial origin for certain physical traits, such as the cleft palate (an opening in the roof of the mouth). Mengele would

also have a third article eventually published, titled "Hereditary Transmission of Fistulae Auris," an abnormal opening in the cartilage of the ear.

The year 1938 also saw the threat of war loom ominously over Europe. Hitler had already taken steps to put into effect his plan to dominate Europe and bring Germany back to what he believed was its rightful place as a world power. As preparation for the coming battle Mengele began three months of basic training with the *Wehrmacht*, or German regular army, in October. He was assigned to the Snalfedon-Tirol

29

mountain region. His training there with the specially trained light-infantry regiment included mountain climbing and skiing. While in the Tirol, he had a problem with his unit's commanding

By 1938 Adolf Hitler had invaded a number of neighboring countries and was preparing for war with the rest of Europe.

officer, for whom he had developed an intense dislike. The personality clash between the two eventually resulted in a physical confrontation. Mengele's experience convinced him that he had no future with the *Wehrmacht*. When war eventually broke out, he would opt instead to join the Waffen SS, an elite fighting corps within the SS itself.

Taking a Wife

After returning to Frankfurt following his training with the *Wehrmacht*, Mengele and Irene Schoenbein made plans to wed in 1939. His parents, however, were less than thrilled with his intended wife. They believed the well-educated Irene was too independent to become a traditional German housewife. Even more important to Walburga, she was Lutheran rather than Catholic.

Despite his parents' objections, Mengele was determined to marry his great love. Before he could do so, however, a complete check of her background had to be made by the Central Office for Race and Resettlement in order to determine if she was genetically "pure."

Irene's great-grandfather was Harry Lyons Dumler, an American diplomat who served at the U.S. consulate at Nice. There had long been suspicions that he was not the father of his wife's son (Irene's grandfather). If the boy was, in fact, illegitimate, it was possible that his biological father might have been Jewish. A thorough investigation failed to settle the question, but testimonials from friends of the prospective bride convinced the Central Office that the couple should be allowed to marry. Because her pure Aryan blood could not be verified, however, Mengele was denied a place within the pages of the *Sippenbuch*, or Kinship Book. This honor was reserved for those who could prove pure Aryan ancestry at least since 1750.

The Winds of War

Josef and Irene were married in July 1939. They took up residence in the Sachsenhausen section of Frankfurt, just south of the Main River and a short walk from the Institute for Heredity and Eugenics where Mengele worked as an assistant physician. (Ironically their home was at 30 Paul Erlichstrasse, a street named for the Jewish Nobel Prize winner.) Little more than a month later, World War II began with Germany's invasion of Poland. Mengele was anxious to be called to action, eager to serve in what he called the "last desperate fight of the German nation for its endangered existence."[16]

Mengele's first posting came in the summer of 1940. He joined a regular army unit in Kassel as a medical officer and remained there for one month. He also spent time in occupied Poland with the Genealogical Section of the Race and Resettlement Office. There he served in

an administrative position reviewing applications for German citizenship from the thousands of people living in the surrounding area. Mengele and other doctors assigned to the office conformed to SS leader Heinrich Himmler's four-point program, which was as follows:

(1) The annexed territories were to be thoroughly cleansed of non-Germans; (2) persons claiming any German blood would be classified according to documentary evidence first, and lacking that, by racial examination; those in doubtful categories as well as "renegade" [anti-Nazi or "Polish minded"] Germans would be segregated and subjected to special conditions to ensure "reeducation and good behavior"; (3) persons exhibiting Germanic features would also undergo racial examinations to determine if their ancestors had been "Polanized"; positive cases would be removed from Poland for better re-Germanization in the Reich proper; (4) similar procedures would be carried out upon orphans from Polish orphanages as well as children coming under public care.[17]

In August Mengele joined the Waffen SS as an *Untersturmführer*, or sublieutenant. He did not see battlefield action until he was sent to the Ukrainian front the following June. He was an excellent soldier and earned the praise of his superiors. Within days he was awarded the Iron Cross Second Class for his bravery on the battlefield.

In January 1942 Mengele joined the SS Viking Division (a highly regarded unit, and the only German armed forces armored tank division comprising foreign troops) behind Soviet lines as a field physician. Since there was neither enough equipment nor medication to keep all the wounded alive, one of Mengele's duties was selecting which soldiers would be treated and which would be left to die. Although he hated to do so, he performed this job as a dedicated soldier. It was a foreshadowing of the selection responsibilities he would perform at Auschwitz that would earn him such notoriety in the future.

In July Mengele's division moved up to the front where it engaged in a furious battle that lasted five days. He performed admirably under fire and was even awarded the Iron Cross First Class for pulling two wounded German soldiers from a burning tank under enemy fire and administering first aid to them. He was also awarded the Black Badge for the Wounded and the Medal for the Care of the German People.

Mengele's battlefield service ended in late 1942 when he was wounded and declared unfit for combat. He was assigned to a desk job at the Race and Resettlement Office at its headquarters in Berlin and promoted to the rank of *Haupsturmführer*, or captain.

Reunited with von Verschuer

Earlier in the summer of 1942, Professor von Verschuer, Mengele's mentor in Frankfurt, took over the position of director at the prestigious Kaiser Wilhelm Institute in Berlin. His duties involved overseeing research dealing with questions of racial purity. Von Verschuer undoubtedly intended to have Mengele join him there. In a January 1943 letter, he told one of his colleagues that "my assistant Mengele has been transferred to a post in Berlin so that in his free time he can work at the Institute."[18]

In his capacity as one of the most prominent Nazi scientists, von Verschuer was certainly aware of Hitler's Final Solution policy that had recently been formalized in Berlin. The policy was the Nazi code name for the plan to physically liquidate all European Jews. Von Verschuer was also aware of the research being undertaken in the large concentration camps that had been built to hold Jewish prisoners. The camps presented ideal opportunities for genetic experiments that could be carried out on human subjects. Medical projects of various kinds had been under way since 1939. Human subjects had been infected with diseases such as typhoid fever, tuberculosis, diphtheria, cholera, smallpox, yellow fever, and influenza in an effort to learn how to control them.

Experiments were also being undertaken to find efficient methods of mass sterilization.

For Mengele and von Verschuer some of the most exciting work of all was being done at the concentration camp at Auschwitz. There Dr. Horst Schumann was exposing inmates to high doses of radiation in an attempt to see if the method could be used for sterilizing undesirables. Auschwitz was larger than the other camps, with ten thousand new inmates arriving every day. The chance to experiment on men, women, and children of various racial groups was unprecedented.

It is almost certain that von Verschuer convinced Mengele to pursue this unique opportunity to carry on his research. Only there would he have an almost unlimited supply of subjects of various races on which to carry out experiments. Mengele applied for a position at the German *Konzentrationslager*, or concentration camp, in southern Poland. In May 1943 he received his posting to Auschwitz.

Heinrich Himmler created Dachau, the first Nazi concentration camp.

The First Concentration Camps

The first concentration camp, Dachau, was created by Heinrich Himmler almost as soon as the Nazis rose to power in 1933. It was a place where political prisoners were to be "concentrated" and held.

By the middle and late 1930s, the categories of inmates had been expanded to include those considered habitual criminals, antisocial elements (such as Gypsies, vagrants, prostitutes, drunkards, and beggars), homosexuals, Jehovah's Witnesses, and Jews.

Within a short period of time, the Nazis built fifty camps in and around Germany. The most infamous of all was the killing center at Auschwitz.

Auschwitz

On April 27, 1940, Heinrich Himmler had given orders for a large new concentration camp to be established near the town of Oswiecim in Poland, which the Germans had taken over the previous September. It was to be located in a sparsely inhabited region, approximately thirty-eight miles west of Krakow. A rail line running from Vienna to Warsaw lay nearby, making

The Wannsee Conference

On January 20, 1942, one of the most infamous meetings in history took place at a lakeside villa in the wealthy Berlin district of Wannsee. Gathered at the serene setting were fifteen high-ranking members of the Nazi Party and the SS, together with leading ministerial officials. The purpose of the meeting was to discuss what was euphemistically referred to as the "Final Solution of the Jewish Question"—the systematic extermination of all European Jews.

The conference was organized by Reinhard Heydrich, chief of the German State Police and of the Security Service of the SS. The minutes of the hour-and-a-half-long meeting were written by Adolf Eichmann, head of the Department for Jewish Affairs. The long-standing "Jewish Question" was whether Jews should be assimilated into the countries where they lived or have their own separate nation. The Nazis' answer called for the "evacuation … to the East" of some 11 million Jews.

Although the minutes of the meeting make no mention of genocide, there is little question as to the Final Solution's intent. After Eichmann was apprehended in 1960, he was put on trial in Jerusalem. According to Patricia Brennan's article in the *Washington Post*, Eichmann testified during the trial that "the gentlemen convened their session, and then in very plain terms—not in the language that I had to use in the minutes, but in absolutely blunt terms—they addressed the issue, with no mincing of words....

"The discussion covered killing, elimination, and annihilation."

Concentration Camps Throughout Europe

FINLAND

NORWAY

SWEDEN

USSR

ESTONIA

North Sea

LATVIA

DENMARK

Baltic Sea

LITHUANIA

Neuengamme

Sachsenhausen-
Oranienburg

EAST
PRUSSIA

Bergen-Belsen

Ravensbrück

POLAND

NETHERLANDS

Stutthof

GERMANY

Treblinka

Chelmno

Gross-Rosen

Sobibor

BELGIUM

Majdanek

Mittelbaudora

Auschwitz-
Birkenau

Belzec

Flossenbürg

Zweiler-
Struthof

Theresienstadt

CZECHOSLOVAKIA

FRANCE

Mauthausen

SWITZERLAND

AUSTRIA

HUNGARY

ROMANIA

Dachau

ITALY

YUGOSLAVIA

Adriatic
Sea

BULGARIA

Mediterranean Sea

- ● Detention camps/Gestapo prisons
- ◉ Large-scale labor camps
- ▣ Large-scale extermination camps

it convenient for the transport of inmates.

The camp was originally intended for Polish political prisoners, whom the Nazis began transporting in June. In less than a year, nearly eleven thousand inmates were impounded in the twenty-eight buildings of the original camp (Auschwitz I). With more room needed for the increasing number of

Gypsy prisoners at Dachau line up for a medical inspection.

Jews and other European prisoners, plans were made for the construction of another site at Birkenau, less than two miles away. This site—Auschwitz II, or Birkenau—was established in October 1941 as a *Vernichtungslager*, or extermination camp. This is where Mengele was stationed. A third camp—Auschwitz III, or Monowitz—was created as an *Arbeitslager*, or work camp, the following May.

The Extermination Factory

Auschwitz-Birkenau was by far the largest of the Nazi extermination centers. Extending for miles in all directions, the camp could hold well over one hundred thousand inmates. As camp commandant Rudolf Hoess noted in his autobiography, "The numbers envisaged were at this time something entirely new in the history of concentration camps. At that time a camp containing ten thousand persons was considered exceptionally large."[19]

The wide-ranging site was enclosed by barbed wire and electrified fences and patrolled by vicious guard dogs. Watchtowers were staffed by SS men who stood guard with machine guns and automatic rifles, ready to shoot anyone who made any attempt to escape. The camp contained five crematoria and gas chambers, whose red brick chimneys rose into the sky, belching forth black smoke that filled the air with a putrid odor. (When Mengele's wife visited him in late

The Kaiser Wilhelm Society

In June 2001 Hubert Markl, president of the Max Planck Society, apologized on behalf of its forerunner, the Kaiser Wilhelm Society, to the survivors of concentration camp experiments. As he said, "There is scientific evidence proving beyond the shadow of a doubt that directors and employees at Kaiser Wilhelm Institutes co-masterminded and sometimes even actively participated in the crimes of the Nazi regime."

Included in the Confession of Historical Responsibility, found on the Max Planck Society website, was a description of Mengele's involvement:

Some scientists at Kaiser Wilhelm Institutes made use of the opportunity to conduct morally unrestricted research at Nazi coercive institutions such as psychiatric clinics or the Auschwitz concentration camp. Among them was Otmar von Verschuer, who, beginning in 1942, headed up projects in so-called twins research at Berlin's Kaiser Wilhelm Institute for Anthropology, Human Genetics and Eugenics. Concentration camp doctor Josef Mengele was neither employed by nor working on behalf of the Kaiser Wilhelm Society. He was a protege of Otmar von Verschuer's, under whom he earned his doctorate in 1938 at the University of Frankfurt. Even after that, the two stayed in close contact. Today, it is safe to say that von Verschuer knew of the crimes being committed in Auschwitz and that he—together with some of his employees and colleagues—used them for his purposes.

August 1943, she asked him what the horrible stench was. "Don't ask me about this," he is reported to have said.[20] Years later their son Rolf would maintain that this was the moment when his mother first began to have doubts about her husband's duties at Auschwitz.)

Although extermination was its primary purpose, Auschwitz also served as a slave-labor camp. Since the war effort required a great deal of manpower, the camp provided a pool of workers for munitions factories and many other German companies.

The inmates at Auschwitz were housed in the most wretched accommodations imaginable. Prisoners slept on wooden planks in triple-tiered bunks rather than in beds. They were fed the most meager of meals, consisting of watered-down soup for lunch and a half pound or so of moldy bread for dinner. With a daily diet of less than seven hundred calories, inmates burned off fat and muscle in no time at all and quickly

Concentration camp inmates were fed meager rations, and they quickly became emaciated. Most prisoners died within months of arriving at the camps.

became emaciated. It was rare for workers to survive for more than a couple of months on such rations. Those who did last longer did so by stealing things that could be traded for food.

Sanitary conditions in the barracks were abominable. As one inmate re-called, "Lice were everywhere, even on the crust of bread we ate. Our gray horse blankets were totally infested. If you looked closely, you could see that the blankets were absolutely crawling with them."[21] Since there was no septic system to dispose of waste, prisoners had to use ditches in the ground as their toilet facilities. The water supply quickly became polluted, and diseases such as typhus were rampant.

In contrast the quarters reserved for Mengele and the other SS officers were more than simply tolerable. They lived outside the electrified fences and had access to a bakery, slaughterhouse, and sausage factory. There was even a swimming pool for use during the hot summer months.

It was into this world that Mengele entered in May of 1943, passing through a gate adorned with the sign *Arbeit Macht Frei* (Work Brings Freedom).

Chapter Three

The Angel of Death

Mengele's mission at Auschwitz was to support the Nazis' ultimate goal of purifying and improving the German race. In pursuit of this objective, he was given the authority to make life or death decisions affecting thousands of prisoners detained at Auschwitz. His obsession with his work earned him a reputation as a cold-blooded killer who became known as the Angel of Death.

Camp Doctor

Mengele was one of twenty-two camp doctors at Auschwitz. He was the only one, however, to have been decorated for his service on the battlefield. He wore his Iron Cross and other medals proudly on his uniform. This immediately set him apart from the other doctors in the camp.

Mengele also distinguished himself from the others through his attention to his work. He did not hesitate to take on new projects and additional responsibilities, doing so with a gusto not seen in the others. His devotion to Nazi precepts and philosophy was carried out with an unsurpassed thoroughness and ruthlessness, which earned him the respect and appreciation of his superiors.

A Ruthless Efficiency

Mengele demonstrated his callous attitude soon after he arrived at Auschwitz. Because of the horrid sanitary conditions and scarcity of clean water, typhus was a common affliction among the inmates. In the past, camp doctors had been unable to control the disease. Mengele's solution to the problem was to send 507 Gypsy men and 528 Gypsy women suspected of having the disease to the gas chamber. His indifference to taking their lives was owed to his belief that Gypsies, like Jews, were subhuman and unworthy of life.

Later that same year, Mengele demonstrated his efficiency when another outbreak struck some seven thousand prisoners at the women's camp at Birkenau. He ordered an entire block of six hundred Jewish women to the gas chamber and then had their quarters fumigated and sanitized. He had the women from the next block cleaned and disinfected and their clothes and other belongings destroyed. He then transferred them to the clean block. He continued in this manner until all of the blocks had been disinfected and the disease eliminated.

Selektions

Mengele's reputation and utter disregard for life was solidified with his work presiding over *selektions*, the process that determined which of the incoming inmates would live and which would die. The trains overflowing with incoming Jewish deportees reached Auschwitz three or four times a day—and at night—arriving from various countries within Nazi rule. When the doors to the cattle cars filled with their human cargo opened, those who disembarked were rushed along by SS soldiers hollering, *"Raus, raus!"* ("Out,

out!"). The transportees, unaware of their fate, rarely offered any resistance. They believed they had been sent for the purpose of resettlement. The real reason for the camp's existence—as a "death factory"—was well hidden by the Nazis.

The transportees were separated into two lines—one for men and one for women—at the arrival ramp. For many it would be the last time they would see their loved ones. The lines were met by the camp doctors on duty. The officer in charge explained that they would be separated into two groups. Those qualified

Mengele (pictured) decided the fate of prisoners upon their arrival at Auschwitz.

A train full of prisoners arrives at a concentration camp. Prisoners were immediately separated into groups of those physically able to work and those unfit to do so.

to do work would form a column to the right; those deemed unable to work—including the elderly, the young, and women with small children—would form another column to the left. Those who could not work, they were told, would go the compounds where the inmates lived to set up housekeeping. In reality they were sent directly to the gas chambers.

Gas rather than shooting had been chosen as the method of execution because of the number of inmates involved. As Hoess explained, "it would have been absolutely impossible by shooting to dispose of the large numbers of people that were expected, and it would have placed too heavy a burden on the SS men who had to carry it out, especially because of the women and children among the victims."[22] On some occasions, however, there were relatively few people to be executed. Rather than waste gas to kill them, those prisoners would be brought to an *Unterscharführer*, or sergeant, who would systematically shoot them in the neck.

Rationalizing Murder

Generally, it was Mengele's policy to kill mothers along with their children. A compilation called The Facilitator *quotes the remarkable piece of reasoning Mengele used in order to rationalize the murders of mothers and their newborn infants:*

When a Jewish child is born, or when a woman comes to the camp with a child already, I don't know what to do with the child. I can't set the child free because there are no longer any Jews who live in freedom. I can't let the child stay in the camp because there are no facilities in the camp that would enable the child to develop normally. It would not be humanitarian to send a child to the ovens without permitting the mother to be there to witness the child's death. That is why I send the mother and child to the gas ovens together.

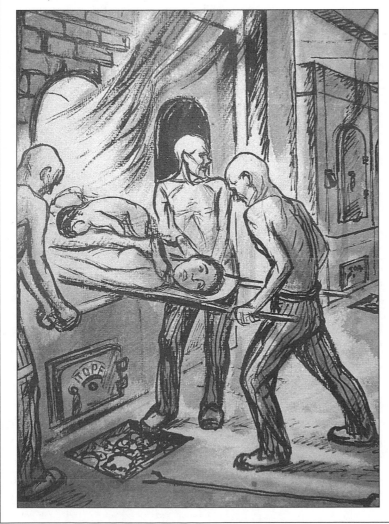

Jewish prisoners insert the bodies of a mother and child into a furnace at Auschwitz. Mengele typically ordered that mothers and their children be put to death together.

Those consigned to death had to undress in front of the gas chambers, as they were told they would have to shower and be disinfected. Mengele would occasionally have the women undress and parade in front of him in the nude. He would then ask them intimate questions about their personal lives to further degrade them.

They were then herded into the so-called bath, and the doors were closed. (Dummy showerheads made of metal were mounted on the ceiling to delude those entering the chamber into believing they were in a shower room.) Zyklon B, which produced hydrogen cyanide gas, was then introduced into the chamber. Death usually occurred within fifteen minutes. Mengele or another doctor assigned to duty would peer into the room through a peephole to see if there were any signs of life. If not, he would give the signal to turn on the fans to disperse the gas. After several more minutes, the doors to the chamber were opened and a special *Kommando*, or work crew, removed the bodies, which were then taken to the furnaces for cremation. When enough ashes were gathered from the oven, they were removed, pulverized, and loaded into trucks. Approximately once a week, the trucks would be taken to the nearby river, and their cargo thrown in. As William Shirer reported in *The Rise and Fall of the Third Reich*, the remains were occasionally disposed of in other ways. "There was testimony at the Nuremberg trials," wrote

Shirer, "that the ashes were sometimes sold as fertilizer. One Danzig firm . . . constructed an electrically heated tank for making soap out of human fat."[23]

Those transportees whose lives were spared—between 10 to 30 percent of each trainload—were sent to an area called the quarantine. A registration number was tattooed onto their left forearm with a searing metal rod. Their hair was shaved off, and they were given striped prison clothes to wear before being sent to their barracks. Some of these would eventually become subjects of Mengele's evil experiments.

Since each trainload brought more healthy laborers, selections were also made within the camp each day at roll call, which might occur at any time, to weed out the weaker, more emaciated workers. The detainees were made to stand for hours on end, in the freezing cold and snow, often without having slept. The ones who were not strong enough to endure the cold were sent off to be gassed.

Mengele occasionally resorted to haphazard, less precise methods in order to determine who would live and who would die. In October 1943, on the Jewish holy day of Yom Kippur, he went to a soccer field on which some two thousand young boys were being held. Mengele instructed one of the guards to nail a piece of wood onto one of the goalposts at a certain height. He then commanded the boys to walk underneath. Those whose heads did not reach

Naked women and children are lined up for execution. The Nazis used a variety of methods to humiliate, torture, and kill prisoners.

the level of the marker—about half of them—were sent off to be gassed.

An Elegant Figure

Many of the doctors assigned to the selection process at the ramp did their work reluctantly, finding it difficult to reconcile the procedure with their role as physicians. Mengele, however, was unlike the others. He performed his duties with the unsympathetic, icy composure expected of an SS officer. As Dr. Ella Lingens—an Austrian

imprisoned for attempting to hide some Jewish friends—remembered, "Some like Werner Rhöde who hated his work, and Hans König who was deeply disgusted by the job, had to get drunk before they appeared on the ramp. Only two doctors performed the selections without any stimulants of any kind: Dr. Josef Mengele and Dr. Fritz Klein. Dr. Mengele was particularly cold and cynical."[24]

Dressed in his neatly pressed, immaculate, tight-fitting SS uniform

45

The Death Factories of Auschwitz

The death factories at the main camp of Auschwitz and Birkenau where Mengele worked comprised the following facilities:

Main camp, Auschwitz

Crematorium I   Gas chamber, three ovens for 340 bodies

Birkenau

Bunker I   Two gas chambers for 800 persons, disrobing rooms, mass graves

Bunker II   Four gas chambers for 1,200 persons, disrobing rooms, burning pits

Crematoriums   Subterranean installation with five ovens, daily capacity of 1,440
   II and III   bodies, gas chamber for up to 3,000 persons

Crematoriums   Aboveground installation with two ovens, daily capacity of 768
   IV and V   bodies, four gas chambers for approximately 3,000 persons

Ovens like these were used to incinerate the bodies of prisoners put to death.

with white gloves, black boots, and polished cane, Mengele would survey the prisoners at the ramp. Often he would whistle a favorite opera tune from Strauss or Wagner while performing his duties. Dr. Olga Lengyel, another inmate, recalled,

> Day after day he was at his post, watching the pitiful crowd of men and women and children go struggling past, all in the last stages of exhaustion from the inhuman journey in the cattle trucks. He would point with his cane at each person and direct them with one word: "right" or "left." . . . He seemed to enjoy his grisly task.[25]

Although some former inmates recall Mengele as being at every transport, evidence indicates the doctors all took turns on duty at the ramp. He is known to have performed this duty at least seventy-four times. Mengele often appeared at other selections, however, in order to inspect the inmates— particularly twins—who were being saved for his experiments. His constant attendance at the selections where the life and death decisions were made, and the cool efficiency and commitment he had for the job, earned him the nickname of the Angel of Death. (Although its derivation is not clear, it is likely that the name was first applied to Mengele after the war, possibly by an inmate survivor.)

A Streak of Cruelty

For the most part Mengele maintained an impassive, unemotional demeanor. When the mood struck him, however, he could demonstrate a streak of unimaginable cruelty. On one such occasion, he came across a woman who had escaped the gas chamber several times by jumping off the truck that transported the victims. As former inmate Dr. Gisella Perl recalled,

> He grabbed her by the neck and proceeded to beat her head to a bloody pulp. He hit her, slapped her, boxed her, always her head— screaming at her at the top of his voice, "You want to escape, don't you. You can't escape now. This is not a truck, you can't jump. You are going to burn like the others, you are going to croak, you dirty Jew," and he went on hitting the poor unprotected head. As I watched, I saw her two beautiful, intelligent eyes disappear under a layer of blood. Her ears weren't there any longer, maybe he had torn them off. And in a few seconds, her straight, pointed nose was a flat, broken, bleeding mass. I closed my eyes, unable to bear it any longer, and when I opened them up again, Dr. Mengele had stopped hitting her. But instead of a human head, Ibi's tall, thin body carried a round, blood-red object on its bony shoulders, an unrecognizable object, too

horrible to look at; he pushed her back into line. Half an hour later, Dr. Mengele returned to the hospital. He took a piece of perfumed soap out of his bag and, whistling gaily with a smile of deep satisfaction on his face, he began to wash his hands.[24]

Another time one of the Jewish inmates who assisted the Nazis in herding transportees to the gas chambers tried to move some prisoners from the gas chamber line to the labor line. When Mengele found out, he could not contain his fury. He murdered the inmate with his own pistol right on the spot.

On other occasions Mengele is reported to have grabbed a newborn child by the head and thrown it onto a pile of corpses, split an old man's skull by hitting him over the head with an iron bar, and shot prisoners for imagined slights. Perhaps the most horrifying allegation of all is that Mengele once had three hundred children thrown into a fire burning in an open pit. (This was reportedly done when the number of prisoners grew too large to be handled by the gas chambers.) As former Russian inmate Annani Silovich Pet'ko related:

A large group [of SS officers] arrived on motorcycles, Mengele among them. . . . Upon arriving they circled the flames; it burned horizontally. . . . After a while trucks arrived, dump trucks, with children inside. There were about ten of these trucks. After they had entered the yard an officer gave an order and the trucks backed up to the fire and they started throwing those children right into the fire, into the pit. The children started to scream; some of them managed to crawl out of the burning pit; an officer walked around it with sticks and pushed back those who managed to get out. Hoess and Mengele were present and were giving orders.[27]

Doubling

Despite displaying such unimaginably cruel behavior, Mengele was also capable of showing kindness and affection in almost the same breath. One example occurred with a group of Jewish children who were suffering from painful mouth ulcers. Mengele went to great lengths to find a cure to relieve the children's suffering. When they recovered, however, he sent some of them directly to the gas chambers.

This confusing display of contradictory behavior was called "doubling" by Robert Jay Lifton, a professor of psychiatry and psychology at the City University of New York. In "doubling," a person has two personalities, each of which is capable of acting on its own.

Jewish children stand behind barbed wire at Auschwitz. Mengele ordered the deaths of thousands of children, killing many himself.

According to Lifton, the Nazi doctors underwent a habituation to evil.

Before going to Auschwitz, they were ordinary people doing their jobs and living their normal lives. At Auschwitz they ran the entire inhumane killing process, with their selections determining who would live and who would die. When they went home to their families on weekends or on leaves, however, they returned to their non-Auschwitz lives as ordinary fathers and husbands. Back at the concentration camp, they reverted to their Auschwitz selves.

Although many of Mengele's acts seemed to be motivated by sadism, that is not generally believed to be the case. Most witnesses indicated that he did not seem to get pleasure from the suffering he inflicted on others, but rather appeared totally oblivious or indifferent to it. As Dr. Tobias Brocher, a Menninger Foundation psychoanalyst explained, "He didn't take pleasure in inflicting pain, but in the power he exerted by being the man who had to decide between life and death within the ideology of a concentration camp doctor."[28]

The Healer

Mengele also held the power over life and death among those under his med-

Prisoner Doctors

Mengele's assistants in his research were mainly doctors and nurses who had been imprisoned. These inmate-physicians at Auschwitz faced difficult moral dilemmas. As Robert Jay Lifton wrote in *The Nazi Doctors*, "For prisoner doctors to remain healers was profoundly heroic and equally paradoxical: heroic in their combating the overwhelming Auschwitz current of murder; paradoxical in having to depend upon those who had abandoned healing for killing—the Nazi doctors."

Different doctors handled the situation in different ways. Some agreed to collaborate with their captors and do whatever was asked of them simply to stay alive. Others continued to do what they could to alleviate the suffering of patients who would soon be put to death. Still others performed procedures they might normally have found repellent—such as abortions—in order to save the lives of pregnant women who would otherwise have been killed had the Nazis become aware of their condition. The agonizing decisions and moral dilemmas faced by these physicians, causing them daily struggles with their consciences, were unprecedented in medical history.

ical supervision. Prior to arriving at Auschwitz, he had spent a relatively brief part of his career practicing medicine (just the few months at Leipzig and his tour of duty with the Viking Division). Part of his duties at Auschwitz, however, required him to use his skills as a clinical physician.

Very little doctoring of the sick and injured took place in the shacks designated as hospitals. Inmates were treated only to ensure the supply of trained slave labor. Medical supplies and qualified help were in short supply. As often as not, serious illness resulted in the death of the individual. Mengele placed a fourteen-day limit on hospital stays. German companies paid the SS for the labor of the inmates but would only finance two weeks' sick leave for each individual. If a patient was not recovered enough in that time to go back to work, he or she was either gassed or shot.

Much of Mengele's time was spent helping to control contagious diseases, such as typhus, that affected large sectors of the prisoner population. These illnesses proliferated because of the squalid conditions and the presence of millions of fleas and lice. Those suffering from such maladies were put to death as a matter of course in order to prevent further contagion. Because of this, inmate-doctors sometimes conspired to trick Mengele by hiding the true nature of an inmate's disease.

Former inmate-doctor Gisella Perl put the overall atmosphere at the hospital in perspective:

> To a doctor like myself, a hospital is the most sacred place, a sanctuary set aside to provide relief from pain and suffering. Mengele made a sadistic joke out of the hospital. I studied medicine in Germany, and I know that all of the medical students there were instructed on the Hippocratic oath [an oath of ethical professional behavior sworn by new physicians]. I was amazed at how seriously it seemed to be taken. It was like a piece of the Bible, that document. And Mengele, he made a dirty piece of paper of it.[29]

Unwanted Pregnancies

Pregnant women also drew Mengele's attention. Rather than caring for them, however, his interest was far more sinister. Since they were of little value to the workforce, such women were usually marked for death. As he told them, "This is not a maternity ward."[30] He explained away his behavior in what he felt were humanitarian terms: Since there were no facilities where newborns could be taken care of, it was better for all concerned if the women were killed.

At first, Mengele used ruses to separate the pregnant women from the others. One time, according to an inmate-nurse, he addressed the women

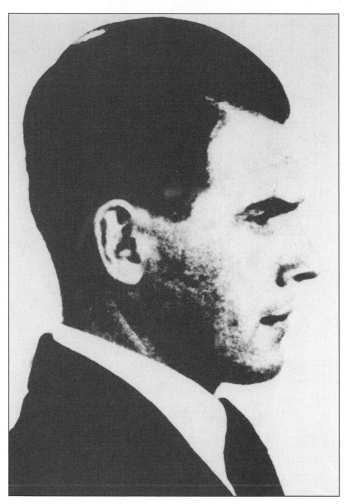

Mengele sent most pregnant women to the gas chambers because they were unable to work.

At other times Mengele made no secret of his intentions. On at least one occasion he is reported to have pushed a pregnant woman to the ground and proceeded to kick her in the stomach until the pregnancy was aborted. Another pregnant woman named Ruth Eliaz somehow escaped Mengele's detection during the selection process. When he realized his error, he allowed her to live. When the baby was born, however, he had the woman's breasts bound so she would not be able to nurse her child. In this way Mengele could see how long the infant could live without food. As the baby grew weaker, a sympathetic nurse gave the mother some morphine and a syringe. She convinced the woman to kill her daughter rather than let the child die by starvation.

Even those not with child were sometimes affected. Auschwitz survivor Judith Yagudah remembered, "My aunt, my mother's sister, was a bit overweight. She had a stomach. Mengele was convinced she was pregnant, and so he sent her to be gassed."[31] When word of Mengele's position on pregnant women became known, they did their best to conceal their condition from him. The Jewish

during roll call and invited any who were pregnant to come forward for lighter duty. The ones who did so were herded into a truck and sent to the gas chambers. Another time the ones who came forward were promised a transfer to another camp with better food. They, too, were sent to their deaths.

inmate-doctors who assisted him often performed secret abortions in an effort to save the women from certain death.

Occasionally, however, Mengele decided to let such women live and carry their children to term. This usually occurred when he planned to use the mother or her offspring as a subject in one of his experiments. For many of these infants, their fate was worse than death.

Chapter Four

EXPERIMENTS IN TERROR

Mengele's stated purpose in going to Auschwitz was to conduct scientific research in human genetics. The availability of twins for such research presented him with an ideal situation. Without the restrictions of the ethical norms that were in existence prior to the Nazis' rise to power, his experiments took on a horrific character, adding to his reputation as an emotionless, cold-blooded fiend.

In von Verschuer's Footsteps

Professor Otmar Freiherr von Verschuer's research on families and twins dated back to the 1920s when he was head of the genetics department at the Kaiser Wilhelm Institute in Berlin. He was convinced that experiments on twins could help scientists make "a reliable determination of what is hereditary in

man."[32] Because of his strict Catholic upbringing and the ethics of the day, his work was based on observation rather than "in vivo" experiments on living subjects.

As von Verschuer's assistant, Mengele, too, became convinced of the value of such studies. He was drawn to Auschwitz for the potential it presented as a research laboratory, with a virtually unlimited supply of subjects. His work there received financial backing authorized by the *Deutsche Forschungsgemeinshaft* (German Research Society). Von Verschuer had applied for assistance, explaining to the council,

My co-researcher in this research is my assistant the anthropologist and physician Mengele. He is serving as *Hauptsturmführer* and camp doctor in the concentration camp Auschwitz. With the permission of the Reichsführer SS [Himmler], anthropological research is being undertaken on the various racial groups in the concentration camp and blood samples will be sent to my laboratory for investigation.[33]

Death-camp survivor Eva Mozes Kor holds a picture of herself and her twin sister. Mengele performed experiments on the twins.

The money was used to outfit a special laboratory in Crematorium 2 at Birkenau. It would be the site of much of Mengele's gruesome work.

"Zwillinge, Zwillinge"

Although Mengele's experiments at Auschwitz touched on a wide variety of disciplines, the common goal joining them was to unlock the secrets that could improve future generations of the Aryan race. Research involving twins played a large part in reaching this objective. Identical twins born from a single egg—and to a lesser extent, fraternal twins—provided the perfect opportunity to examine the effects of heredity and environment. Variables could be manipulated on one twin, while the other acted as a control. Although exact numbers are unavailable, it is estimated that as many as fifteen hundred pairs of twins arrived at Auschwitz over the course of Mengele's time at the camp (May 1943 to January 1945).

Through his experiments Mengele hoped to find a way of improving the Aryan birthrate. As described in a 1981 warrant for Mengele's arrest issued by the West German Prosecutor's Office,

The research into twins occupied a large part of the pseudo experiments of the accused according to the Court's preliminary investigations. This was especially interesting to the Nazi regime, in particular with regard to a desired increase in the birth rate through medically manipulated increase in the number of births of twins.[34]

The Nazis hoped to discover how to produce more Aryan twins in order to increase the population of the super-race.

Mengele's thoughts were always on his research, even while he carried out his responsibilities as selector. He would instruct the SS guards who assisted him to scour the crowds of prisoners for twins. The guards could be heard yelling, *"Zwillinge, zwillinge"* ("Twins, twins") as the inmates marched up the ramp after being transported to the camp. As surviving twin Eva Mozes recalled,

> When the doors to our cattle car opened, I heard SS soldiers yelling, *"Schnell! Schnell!"* ("Faster! Faster!"), and ordering everybody out. My mother grabbed Miriam and me by the hand. She was always trying to protect us because we were the youngest. . . . As I clutched my mother's hand, an SS man hurried by shouting, "Twins! Twins!" He stopped to look at us. Miriam and I looked very much alike. We were wearing similar clothes. "Are they twins?" he asked my mother. "Is that good?" she replied. He nodded yes. "They are twins,"[35] she said.

Mengele's Children

The twins—who came to be known as Mengele's Children—were separated from the rest of the inmate population and sent to Barrack 14 of Camp F in Birkenau. This was reserved for the subjects of Mengele's experiments, which included dwarfs and cripples as well as twins. His subjects received special treatment in the barrack, which was nicknamed the Zoo. In addition to being allowed to keep their hair and some of the belongings they brought with them, they were spared beatings and given extra food to ensure their good health.

Conditions in the children's barrack, however, still left much to be desired. As Eva Mozes Kor recalled,

> The first time I went to use the latrine located at the end of the children's barrack, I was greeted by the scattered corpses of several children lying on the ground. I think that image will stay with me forever. It was there that I made a silent pledge—a vow to make sure that Miriam and I didn't end up on that filthy floor.[36]

The twins were eventually informed as to the fate of the other members of their families in the gas chambers and crematoria. Mengele became a figure of both life and death for the children, having killed their parents but spared their own lives. He would shower them

"Mengele's Children" slept on these wooden bunks in the children's barracks at Birkenau.

with attention and insist they not be abused by the guards. He wanted to be sure they were in the best condition possible for the gruesome experiments that were to come.

Mengele's more human side was most often seen in his interactions with the twins. He could be very warm and affectionate with them, laughing and joking and offering them candy and toys. The youngest even called him Uncle Mengele. It is possible that Mengele's affection for the twins was in part due to the lack of time he was able to spend with his own son, Rolf, whom his wife had given birth to on

The Seven Dwarfs of Auschwitz

Some of Mengele's experiments were conducted on dwarfs. The Ovitz family comprised seven dwarfs and two full-sized sisters. They were a troupe of Jewish traveling musicians who found themselves transported to Auschwitz after Hitler invaded Hungary in March 1944. Intrigued by the possibility of deciphering the secrets of human growth, Mengele intended to greet the dwarfs personally upon their arrival.

Amid the confusion on the receiving ramp, however, the dwarfs were sent directly to the gas chamber. The doors had already closed and the gas had begun to fill the room when Mengele himself came rushing over to claim the family. Saved from execution, the dwarfs became subjects for Mengele's degrading experiments. They managed to survive, however, and when Auschwitz was liberated, they became the only family to emerge intact from the death camp.

March 11, 1944. Mengele's duties at the camp provided him with few opportunities to visit with Irene and Rolf.

As Mengele's favorites the children received better treatment than the other inmates. They were not subjected to beatings and received more food than the others. Since everyone in the camp knew that the children "belonged" to Mengele, they were spared the punishments often meted out to the others. Even the brutal camp guards were afraid to incur the wrath of the terrifying doctor.

Collecting Data

During the preliminary phase of the experiments the children were made to fill out a detailed questionnaire from the Kaiser Wilhelm Institute. The questions concerned their background, health, and physical characteristics such as age, height, weight, hair color, and eye color. One of the older twins in the camp—twenty-nine-year-old Zvi Spiegel—was put in charge of the barrack and came to be known as *Zwillingsvater*, or Twins' Father. One of his duties was to fill out the forms for the younger children. Mengele paid strict attention to such details. Only precise recording of facts and observations would give his work validity and establish his reputation as a research scientist.

A regular part of the twins' routine was daily blood tests. The blood drawn from Mengele's young subjects' fingers, arms, and necks was analyzed in a laboratory near Birkenau. The tests were usually conducted by his assistants—

generally Jewish doctors and nurses who were inmates.

Hair and Eye Color

The Aryan perception of the ideal child was one who had blond hair and blue eyes. Ironically Mengele himself did not fit this stereotype. His dark good looks were more akin to those of the Gypsies, whom he hated as much as the Jews and considered unworthy of life.

Some of Mengele's experiments were aimed at changing the twins' hair color. He would apply different dyes to the children's scalps in an attempt to see if the color could be controlled. Depending on what was used, this often resulted in severe pain for his victims.

Mengele's experiments with eyes were even more grisly. In an attempt to transform brown eyes into the preferred blue, he would either apply drops or use needles to inject methylene blue directly into his subjects' eyeballs. This generally resulted in severe pain and inflammation. After a time the subjects usually returned to normal, but at least one child became blind.

Mengele was also fascinated by a condition known as heterochromia of the iris in which each of a person's eyes is of a different color. This condition seemed to occur more frequently in the Gypsy population. When these children eventually died, Mengele had their eyes removed and sent to Berlin. There Dr. Karin Magnussen, one of von Verschuer's assistants, was involved in a study involving heterochromia.

When Mengele's subjects outlived their usefulness, they were sent to be gassed. Their bodies were moved to the new pathology laboratory in Crematorium 2 where they were dissected. The victims' organs were often saved for future study. One twin—Vera Kriegel—reported seeing a collection of eyes displayed on a wall of a laboratory. "They were pinned up like butterflies," she said. "I thought I was dead and already living in hell."[37]

In the Name of Science

Mengele's attitude towards his work bordered on the obsessive. He was convinced he was among the top research scientists of the day, although many today categorize his work as sloppy and amateurish. Mengele showed no thought or concern for the suffering of his subjects. Sometimes Mengele would cut his subjects and rub sawdust into the open wound. In this way, he sought to duplicate battlefield conditions. Surgery and amputations were often carried out with no anesthetics, while diseases and infections were deliberately brought on in order to see how they affected the subject. Recalls Eva Mozes Kor,

I was given five injections. That evening I developed extremely high fever. I was trembling. My arms and my legs were swollen, huge size. Mengele and Dr. Konig and three other doctors came in the next morning. They looked at my fever chart, and Dr. Mengele said, laughingly, "Too bad, she is so young. She has only two weeks to live."[38]

Many of Mengele's experiments were bizarre to say the least. In one study female twins were given blood transfusions from male twins to see their reaction. Another saw him force one pair of twins to have sex with another in order to see if the union could produce other twins. Other atrocities committed in the name of science included castrating males, cutting the breasts off females, and submitting subjects to electrical stimulation and radiation.

One of the most grotesque experiments of all concerned two children, one of whom had a hunchback. After they were taken away from the others, inmate Vera Alexander recalled, "Two or three days later, an SS man brought them back in a terrible state. They had been cut. The hunchback was sewn to the other child, back to back, their wrists back to back too. There was a terrible smell of gangrene. The cuts were dirty and the children cried every night."[39]

The Final Stage

The in vivo tests provided Mengele with information that he carefully recorded in his notes. The final stage of the experiments, however—dissecting the subjects in order to examine their internal organs—was the most important step of all in his drive to learn all he could about the twins. After the dissections were completed, various organs were removed, packaged, and sent to Berlin for further study at the Kaiser Wilhelm Institute.

In order for the results of the experiments to be most conclusive, the twins had to die at the same time. This way any differences found could reasonably be attributed to the experiment itself, rather than to age or maturity. Arranging simultaneous deaths at Auschwitz was no problem. As Dr. Miklos Nyiszli (an inmate pathologist under Mengele's supervision who performed many of the dissections) later wrote,

> Where under normal circumstances can one find twin[s] who die at the same place and at the same time? For twins like everyone else are separated by life's varying circumstances. One may die at ten, the other at fifty. In the Auschwitz camp, however, there were several hundred sets of twins and therefore as many possibilities of dissection.[40]

When one twin died as a result of an experiment, Mengele had the other also put to death. It might be done by gassing, shooting, or by injecting chloroform directly into the

C.A.N.D.L.E.S.

Eva Mozes Kor was one of the twins who survived Mengele's horrific experiments at Auschwitz. She became interested in reuniting all those who had passed through Mengele's laboratories and lived. Together with her sister Miriam, she eventually located 120 other surviving Mengele twins.

In 1984 the Kors founded the Children of Auschwitz Nazi Deadly Lab Experiments Survivors (C.A.N.D.L.E.S.). The purpose of the organization was to publicize the plight of those children who had suffered at the hands of the infamous Nazi doctor. The symbol of the group is a split Star of David representing the splitting of the egg that produces twins, surrounded by barbed wire. Two candles in the middle symbolize both the twins and how they hope to illuminate the world to the events that occurred at Auschwitz.

Eva Mozes Kor stands in front of a display at the C.A.N.D.L.E.S. Museum in Terre Haute, Indiana.

heart. Often, Mengele would perform the execution himself. Occasionally he would offer a child sweets to get him or her to go with him to the crematorium. He would then shoot the child in the back of the head along the way. On other occasions he would be the one to administer the injections. He is reported to have once killed fourteen Gypsy twins in this way in a single night. The occasion was described by inmate-physician Miklos Nyiszli:

> In the work room next to the dissecting room, fourteen Gypsy twins were waiting [about midnight one night], guarded by SS men, and crying bitterly. Dr. Mengele didn't say a single word to us and prepared a 10 cc. and 5 cc. syringe. From a box he took evipan, and from another box he took chloroform, which was in 20 cubic-centimeter glass containers, and put these on the operating table. After that, the first twin was brought in . . . a fourteen-year-old girl. Dr. Mengele ordered me to undress the girl and put her on the dissecting table. Then he injected the evipan into her right arm intravenously. After the child had fallen asleep, he felt for the left ventricle of the heart and injected 10 cc. of chloroform. After one little twitch the child was dead, whereupon Dr. Mengele had it

taken into the morgue. In this manner, all fourteen twins were killed during the night.[41]

A Driving Ambition

Mengele carried out his abominable experiments at Auschwitz with an unmatched drive and enthusiasm. He spent all of his spare time in his laboratory, attending to his lurid undertakings. Mengele's colleagues at the camp knew about his obsession with his work, but most later denied being aware of any of the grisly details.

Others, such as survivor Alex Dekel, described Mengele as a madman whose drive for power superseded all else:

> I have never accepted the fact that Mengele himself believed he was doing serious work, not from the slipshod way he went about it. He was only exercising his power. Mengele ran a butcher shop— major surgeries were performed without anesthesia. Once, I witnessed a stomach operation— Mengele was removing pieces from the stomach, but without any anesthetic. Another time, it was a heart that was removed, again, without anethesia. It was horrifying. Mengele was a doctor who became mad because of the power he was given. Nobody ever questioned him—why did this

Mengele conducted some of his experiments on twins in medical rooms like this one at Auschwitz.

one die? Why did that one perish? The patients did not count. He professed to do what he did in the name of science, but it was a madness on his part.[42]

That view, however, was not held by the Chief Doctor's Office. In the August 1944 report made by his garrison commander, Mengele was praised for the vigilance, persistence, and energy with which he carried out his duties at the camp:

Dr. Mengele has an open, honest, solid character. He is absolutely reliable, upright and straightforward. He does not manifest any weakness of character, bad tendencies or cravings. His emotional and physical make-up is outstanding. During his period of service at the Auschwitz concentration camp, he applied his practical and theoretical knowledge to combating severe epidemics. With prudence and persistent energy, and often under the most difficult conditions, he completed every assigned task to the complete satisfaction of his superiors. He showed himself capable of handling any situation. In addition, he used what little free time he had to ardently further his education as an anthropologist. His tactful and modest deportment [conduct] is that of a good soldier. Because of his demeanor, he is especially well liked by his comrades. He treats subordinates with absolute fairness and requisite [necessary] severity, but is nevertheless exceptionally admired and liked. In his behavior,

work record and attitude, Dr. Mengele shows an absolutely solid and mature outlook on life.[43]

Mengele's leadership was commended, and he was recommended for a promotion.

A Visit from Irene

Any hopes Mengele had for a promotion, however, faded soon after. As the Russian army advanced from the east, it became clear to most observers that Germany was losing the war. Mengele's wife noticed a difference in his attitude that showed through in his letters. She

Bars of Soap

For years, survivors of Auschwitz were tormented by nightmares of the horrors that might have befallen their loved ones. As Eva Mozes Kor, who survived Mengele's brutal experiments, related,

"A couple of years after the war, our rabbi in Cluj decided to hold a memorial service for all the Jews from our town who had died in the Holocaust.

The rabbi said that if anyone in the congregation had bars of soap left over from the concentration camp, we should bring it to the temple. He told us it had to be 'buried' because it had been made from human flesh.

It was the first time I had heard that. Before we left the camp, my twin sister and I took whatever we could with us. At a time when goods were scarce, I used the soap all the time.

After the rabbi's address, I felt terrified. I thought, 'Maybe I used soap made from my family.'

For years, I had continuous nightmares. Every night, I dreamt I was washing myself with soap made from my parents or my sister."

made a trip to Auschwitz to try to cheer him up, still unaware, according to her diary, of the gruesome nature of his duties there.

Mengele received permission to take a leave and returned with Irene to Günzburg to visit with his family. It was there that he saw his eight-month-old son, Rolf, for the first time. Although his time away from Auschwitz helped him clear his mind, when he returned in early November, he was still depressed about the direction in which the war was heading.

Evacuation

By the fall of 1944 it had become obvious that it was only a matter of time until the Red Army would reach Auschwitz. On November 26 Himmler sent orders to begin dismantling the camp in order to hide the evidence of what had taken place there over the years. The last gassing at the camp took place that November. When crews were sent to clean out the chimneys at the crematoria, they had to scrape out deposits of human fat eighteen inches thick that had accumulated over the years.

As December came to an end, Mengele ordered his assistants to get his equipment packed away and his records gathered together. Less than three weeks later, in mid-January 1945, Mengele had his records loaded into a waiting car. He departed from Auschwitz one step ahead of the advancing Red Army.

Chapter Five

ESCAPE TO SOUTH AMERICA

With Germany's defeat imminent, Mengele left Auschwitz and made his way back to his homeland. When it became clear that the Allies intended to hunt down those responsible for the atrocities committed during the war, however, he decided to leave Europe. Aided by a network of friends and family, Mengele left Germany to find sanctuary in South America.

On the Move

Mengele joined the growing horde of German soldiers moving west, trying to keep ahead of the Soviet troops. His first stop was at Gross Rosen, another concentration camp approximately two hundred miles to the northwest of Auschwitz in Silesia. Mengele stayed there briefly before continuing his trek westward.

In late February Mengele joined a unit of *Wehrmacht* soldiers as they made their way toward Czechoslovakia. The Russian troops were unstoppable, however, and after two months he was on the move once again. In early May Mengele came across a motorized German field hospital in Saaz in the Sudetenland. It was there that he met up with an old acquaintance, Dr. Hans Otto Kahler. Kahler vouched for his friend with the unit's commanding officer, and Mengele was allowed to join the group.

During Mengele's time with the hospital he formed a close relationship with one of the nurses. He eventually developed complete confidence in her and entrusted her with the safekeeping of his voluminous notes and specimens from Auschwitz. With his capture by the advancing Allied forces becoming more and more a distinct possibility, he knew the records would identify him as one of the doctors at Auschwitz. If the nurse were caught, on the other hand, she would be able to deny that she knew him, or else send those looking for him on false leads.

On the night of May 8, 1945, while the field hospital was crossing over into Saxony (in the territory soon to become East Germany), word reached the unit that the war had ended. Field Marshal Wilhelm Keitel, commander in chief of the High Command of the Armed Forces, had signed an unconditional surrender to the Red Army. Mengele's

German field marshal Wilhelm Keitel signs an unconditional surrender at the Russian headquarters in Berlin.

Evidence

The SS blew up the last crematorium just hours before liberation. When the Soviet army reached Auschwitz on January 27, 1945, only 7,650 sick prisoners remained. In *The Order of Terror: The Concentration Camp*, German sociologist Wolfgang Sofsky gave an account of what else was discovered at Auschwitz. "In the six storerooms still standing," wrote Sofsky, "the liberators found 348,820 men's suits, 836,255 women's dresses and coats, 5,525 pairs of women's shoes, 13,964 rugs, and mountains of children's clothing, spectacles, shaving brushes, and dentures. The rooms of the tannery contained seven tons of human hair."

It is estimated that up to 1.5 million people had been murdered in the camp's gas chambers over the years, making Auschwitz the largest graveyard in the history of humanity.

Allied forces found these piles of clothing at Dachau.

unit was located in a narrow strip of land that separated the American and Soviet forces. Approximately fifteen thousand German soldiers were trapped in the forested region. By mid-June the Americans had entered the area and taken some ten thousand Germans prisoner. Mengele was not among them. Together with his unit, he had avoided capture. As he explained in his autobiography, "With several vehicles and a sanitation unit we formed a column, and with some deception we succeeded in passing through the Americans. We bypassed the subsequent roadblocks and reached Bavarian territory."[44]

Capture—and Release

Mengele's freedom, however, would not last long. With American forces swarming over the area, he was captured soon afterward near the town of Hof. There he was reunited with Kahler and the nurse to whom he had entrusted his Auschwitz records and specimens. As Mengele hoped, she was soon released, taking his treasured notes along with her.

As was to be expected, chaos was the order of the day, as thousands of prisoners had been taken into custody. Although Mengele had given the Americans his real name (possibly because Kahler told him it was dishonorable to use an alias), they did not know he was a member of the SS, since he did not have his blood type tattooed on his chest. He was treated just like any other prisoner, even though he had already been named as a principal war criminal on the first Central Registry of War Criminals and Security Suspects (CROWCASS) list compiled by the Allied High Command in Paris.

Mengele believed his exposure as an Auschwitz doctor was imminent. He became depressed, resigned to his fate. Kahler asked a neurologist friend, Dr. Fritz Ulmann, to see him. Ulmann got him a second set of release papers in Ulmann's name in the hope that it might help him avoid capture in postwar Germany.

To Mengele's surprise and relief, the American forces never became aware of his status as a war criminal. He was eventually set free at the beginning of September 1945 and transported to the Bavarian town of Ingolstadt. Upon his release he headed for the nearby village of Donauworth.

Retrieving His Papers

Donauworth was the home of Dr. Albert Miller, a veterinarian Mengele had known before the war. Miller arranged shelter for his friend, but that very night Miller was brought in for questioning by American troops. Frightened by the close call, Mengele— who had been hiding in a back room of the house at the time—left Donauworth in the middle of the night. He set off for Gera in the hopes of making contact with the nurse who was holding his

Auschwitz records. The journey into the Russian zone would take three weeks.

In the meantime Dr. Miller contacted Mengele's family in Günzburg—and through them his wife Irene in Autenreid—to let them know he was safe. His willingness to help Mengele indicated the attitude prevalent among residents of the region. For the most part they did not believe the charges of atrocities leveled against the Nazis; many thought the horrific stories were primarily Allied propaganda.

After retrieving his materials from his nurse friend in the Russian zone, Mengele set off for Munich. There he was provided with refuge at the home of a pharmacist acquaintance. Over the next few weeks he remained with his friend while recuperating from his experience. His friend did his best to convince him that he would not be able to persuade a court of his innocence (of which he vigorously remained insistent) and that remaining in hiding was the only course of action left open to him.

The Farm Worker

One of Mengele's contacts in Munich was Dr. Ulmann's brother-in-law. He suggested that Mengele look for work in the agricultural area south of the city of Rosenheim, where help was in short supply due to the large number of family members who had been serving in the war. There Mengele would perhaps find safety on one of the region's relatively isolated farms. To further disguise

himself Mengele altered the name on his release papers. "Fritz Ulmann" now became "Fritz Hollmann."

After being turned down at his first two stops, Mengele chanced upon a farm owned by Georg and Maria Fischer. The Fischers grew potatoes and wheat on the property and also raised cows. "Fritz Hollmann" was hired by the Fischers on October 30 at a salary of ten marks a week. Years later Maria Fischer described his duties in an interview: "He was very strong and able. Only he didn't know how to milk. He didn't handle the animals at all, that the farmer would always do himself. Fritz also worked a lot in the fields; he would pull out the potatoes, sort them and carry them to the courtyard, and he worked in our forests, sowing and cutting the trees, and cleaning the trunks. He also cut and loaded hay—in fact he did everything. He was very obliging, never started a fight and was always in a good mood."[45]

The fact that their new hired hand was not used to hard labor helped to convince the Fischers that he had something to hide. Whatever it was, however, was not their concern. All that mattered was that he was a good worker who did not cause trouble.

Contact with Family

One thing that encouraged Mengele during this time was the contact he had with his family. Convinced of his

In the Service of the United States?

Some believe Mengele was helped by U.S. agencies to flee from Europe following the war. These people suggest that he bartered the results of his medical experiments for aid. This belief was fueled by reports of sightings in various American cities. The 1992 U.S. Department of Justice Report to the Attorney General titled In the Matter of Josef Mengele, *however, concludes,*

Review of State Department and U.S. intelligence files permit the confident conclusion that Josef Mengele had no contact with U.S. institutions or personnel following his departure from Europe. Although OSI confirmed that members of the Mengele family did retain ownership interests in U.S. corporations, we know of no reliable information that there was any contact between these entities and Josef Mengele, or that he benefitted from them....

The Department has found no credible evidence that Mengele ever entered the United States, either under his own name or under any of his known aliases....

While it is theoretically possible that Mengele stopped in the United States as a transit passenger on one of his trips to Europe when he lived in South America, the Immigration and Naturalization Service does not maintain records of transit passengers (since, technically, they have not entered the United States).

innocence, they made several trips to Rosenheim to try to keep his spirits up. They also did their best to persuade the authorities that he was dead.

As time went by, Mengele came to believe that the Allies had lost interest in him. He became bolder and bolder, taking chances he had previously avoided, including making a pair of trips to Autenreid to visit his wife and two-year-old son.

Despite the visits life on the run began to wear on Mengele. The time spent apart from Irene put a strain on their marriage. Mengele wanted her to remain at home all the time and not socialize. As a vibrant young woman, this was extremely difficult for her to accept. It was natural that she would cultivate other friendships. When Mengele found out about them, he became insanely jealous. Their meetings often ended in bitter fights that pushed them further apart. Despite this Irene continued to visit him in Rosenheim nearly every other month.

Mengele's hatred of his work on the farm added to his joyless outlook. Although he performed his chores without complaint, he considered picking potatoes and cutting hay degrading for a man with his education. It would not be long before further news added to his depression.

The Nuremberg Trials

The extent of the atrocities committed by the Nazis during the war was not fully comprehended until the concentration camps were liberated by Allied troops. After the war in Europe ended in May 1945, the victorious Allied governments agreed that it was necessary to punish those responsible. As U.S. Supreme Court Justice Robert Jackson would later say, "The wrongs which we seek to condemn and punish have been so calculated, so malignant and so devastating that civilization cannot tolerate their being ignored because it cannot survive their being repeated."[46]

With this in mind the four main Allied nations—the United States, Great Britain, France, and the Soviet Union—set up the International Military Tribunal (IMT). Prosecutors for the four countries issued indictments against twenty-two high-level Nazi officials on four counts: conspiracy to wage aggressive war, waging aggressive war (crimes against peace), war crimes, and crimes against humanity. Six Nazi organiza-

tions—the SS, the *Gestapo*, the Corps of the Political Leaders of the Nazi Party, the SA, the Reich Cabinet (*Reichsregierung*), and the General Staff and High Command of the German Forces—were also indicted. In November 1945 the first international war crimes trial began in Nuremberg, Germany. The following month the Allies announced that retribution would not be limited to the twenty-two Nazis being tried at Nuremberg. Other war criminals would also be brought up on charges in the courts of the individual countries involved.

Mengele followed the proceedings at Nuremberg through local newspaper accounts. He soon learned that his name had been mentioned in court for the first time. During the proceedings on April 15, 1946, camp commandant Rudolf Hoess was questioned about his knowledge of medical experiments carried out on concentration camp internees. Replied Hoess, "Medical experiments were carried out in several camps. For instance in Auschwitz there were experiments on sterilization carried out by Professor Klaubert and Dr. Schumann; also experiments on twins by SS medical officer Dr. Mengele."[47]

The Doctors Trial

Within a short time many of the doctors sought by the Allies were apprehended and put on trial. The death

Guarded by military police, eight Nazi officials (seated in box) are tried at Nuremberg. Mengele closely followed the events at Nuremberg.

sentences carried out against several of his colleagues at Auschwitz further added to Mengele's negative frame of mind. Any hopes he harbored of being able to convince a court of his innocence were quickly fading.

That December the Americans brought twenty-three leading German physicians and doctors to court. They were charged with conspiracy, war crimes, crimes against humanity, and membership in criminal organizations in what became known as the Doctors Trial. Of those found guilty of the charges, seven were sentenced

to death while five others received sentences of life in prison. The verdicts were particularly significant for Mengele since many of the experiments described during the proceedings were similar to ones he had carried out at Auschwitz.

Covering the Trail

Although Mengele had always maintained that his work at Auschwitz was justified, his family realized his capture would mean his execution. His father in Günzburg and Irene in Autenreid made a concerted effort to convince

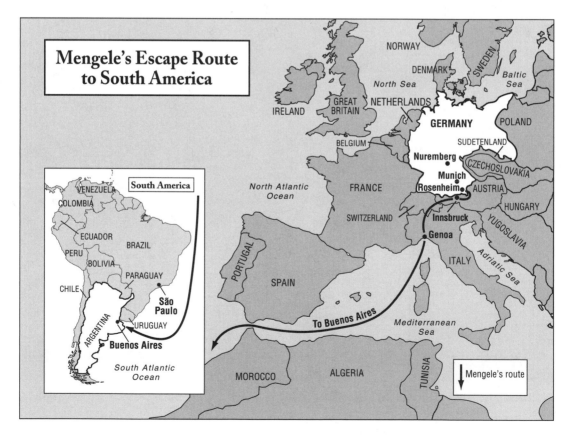

Mengele's Escape Route to South America

the authorities that he was missing and most likely dead.

In part because of his family's assertions and in part due to confusion and disorganization among the American authorities, efforts to find Mengele were uninspired and unproductive. Amazingly he lived in the U.S. occupation zone for four years following his release in 1945 and never was in serious danger of being found.

The Decision to Leave

By the fall of 1948, Mengele had tired of his life under cover in Germany. He longed to make a new start for himself someplace where he did not have to worry constantly about being followed. He decided to leave Germany for South America. Argentina was his destination of choice as it had a large German community that had been established there before the war. There was a good deal of pro-Nazi sentiment in the country, and many Nazi war criminals had already relocated there.

Another factor entering into Mengele's decision concerned his father's farm equipment company. At that time the company had no branches in Argentina. If Mengele went to live there, he would be able to cultivate leads and perhaps help expand the firm's business.

Part of Mengele's plan was to send for Irene and Rolf to join him after he got settled in Buenos Aires, the country's capital and one of the most modern cities on the continent. Irene would not agree to it, however. She did not want to move so far away from her family and the European culture she so dearly loved.

A Close Call

Mengele began his journey in the spring of 1949. With money provided by his family, he traveled by train to Innsbruck, Austria, and then on to Steinach near the Italian border. After crossing over into Italy, he made his way toward Genoa, where he was booked on the *North King*. Passage for Mengele had been booked under the name Helmut Gregor. The ship was scheduled to sail for Buenos Aires on May 25.

Along the way Mengele was contacted by several people who supplied him with money, a German identity card, and a suitcase full of his specimens from Auschwitz. Although it is not known for certain, it is possible these people were members of the *Organization de Ehemaligen SS-Angehorigen* (ODESSA). This group of former SS members set up a network to help war criminals escape from Germany. Another group with similar goals was *Spinne*, or Spider, comprising SS internees in Allied prisoner of war (POW) camps.

Traveling as Gregor, Mengele made it to Genoa needing only an Italian exit visa to complete the last step of his journey. Unfortunately the corrupt official who was Mengele's contact at the immigration department was on vacation. With three days left until his boat was due to sail, Mengele tried to bribe the official in charge but was unsuccessful. The immigration department realized his identification papers were false and placed him under arrest. He was held for three weeks while being interrogated. Believing the *North King* had already left, Mengele again became depressed.

Just when he had lost all hope of escaping, the corrupt official returned from vacation. Mengele was at last granted his exit permit and set free. In another stroke of good luck, he found the *North King* still in port. Mengele boarded the ship and in mid-July 1949 set sail for Buenos Aires.

A New Life as Helmut Gregor

After four weeks at sea the *North King* docked at Buenos Aires harbor on August 26. Mengele stepped off the ship to begin a new life in Argentina as Helmut Gregor. Upon his arrival he was faced with several minor problems, but for the most part his time in Argentina was uneventful. The hunt for him had cooled down, and he was able to live his life in relative comfort.

For a while Mengele was employed as a wool comber and a carpenter. He also worked as a representative for the family business, selling farm machinery to Argentine customers. He took up residence in the well-kept Florida section of Buenos Aires and partook of the many cultural resources the city had to offer.

The biggest disappointment of this period of Mengele's life was the failure of his wife and son to join him. Irene had moved to Freiburg, several hundred miles from Günzburg, and began seeing a man named Alfons Hackenjos. On one of Karl Mengele's visits to Buenos Aires in 1954 he informed his son that Irene wanted a divorce. Mengele had no choice but to agree. The marriage was formally ended on March 25 of that year.

An Arranged Marriage

It was not long before Mengele's father tried to persuade his son to remarry. The girl he had in mind for Josef was Martha Mengele, the widow of his youngest son, Karl Jr., who had died several years before. Rather than being interested in his son's happiness, however, Karl Sr.'s desire for the match had a more selfish motive. If Martha married Josef, control of the business in Günzburg would remain totally in family hands. If she married outside of the family, her voting rights—inherited from her late husband—might be influenced by an outsider.

Mengele's father arranged for the couple to meet in Switzerland in 1956. Mengele obtained a passport and made the trip in March. There he met Martha, her son Karl Heinz, and his own son, Rolf. Mengele was introduced to the boys as their long-lost

Mossad

An organization now called Mossad (short for Ha-Mossad le-Modiin ule-Tafkidim Meyuhadim, or the Central Institute for Intelligence and Special Tasks) was established in April 1951 by then Israeli prime minister David Ben-Gurion. As its mandate, Ben-Gurion stated, "For our state which since its creation has been under siege by its enemies, intelligence constitutes the first line of defense … we must learn well how to recognize what is going on around us."

Headquartered in Tel Aviv, the agency employs approximately 1,200 people. It is responsible for the collection of intelligence, covert operations in foreign countries, and counterterrorism. One of its most publicized activities was tracking down Nazi war criminals such as Adolf Eichmann and Josef Mengele.

Mossad comprises eight departments, including the following:

Collections Department, the largest of the eight, is responsible for espionage operations.

Political Action and Liaison Department conducts political activities and liaison with friendly foreign intelligence services and with nations with which Israel does not have normal diplomatic relations.

Special Operations Division (Metsada) conducts highly sensitive assassination, sabotage, paramilitary, and psychological warfare projects.

LAP (Lohamah Psichlogit) Department is responsible for psychological warfare, propaganda, and deception operations.

Research Department is responsible for intelligence production.

Technology Department is responsible for the development of advanced technologies for support of Mossad operations.

David Ben-Gurion established Mossad in 1951.

Uncle Fritz. (Rolf had been told his father was a war hero who had been killed seeing action on the eastern front. He would not find out that "Uncle Fritz" was actually his father until some time later.) That October Martha and her son moved to Argentina. She and Mengele eventually married in 1958.

By the mid-1950s, interest in Mengele had died down considerably. In a bold move he disposed of his identity as Gregor and began living under his own name. After marrying Martha, he invested in a pharmaceutical company called Fadro Farm KGSA with his father's backing. The company manufactured drugs and medical supplies and helped him provide his family with a good living. After thirteen years on the run, prospects for Mengele's future were beginning to appear brighter. It would not be long, however, before all that changed.

Chapter Six

CHASING SHADOWS

Mengele lived the life of a fugitive in South America, constantly looking over his shoulder for pursuers both real and imagined. With help from his family and friends in Germany he managed to stay one step ahead of those looking for him. He took his secrets to the grave with him, frustrating those who spent a good portion of their lives trying to bring the Angel of Death to justice.

A New Threat

Hermann Langbein, a former political prisoner at Auschwitz, had come across papers that had been filed in Freiburg regarding Mengele's divorce from Irene. Through these he obtained an old address for Mengele in South America. Langbein teamed up with Nazi hunter Simon Wiesenthal to pressure the West German authorities into issuing a warrant for Mengele's arrest. The warrant was issued on June 7, 1959, followed by a request for his extradition from Argentina.

By the time all the paperwork was completed, however, Mengele had been warned of the danger by friends. He signed over power of attorney to Martha, in case decisions had to be made while he was not around. He then left for Paraguay where he was trying to sell a new piece of farm equipment manufactured by the Günzburg firm. The country was ruled by Alfredo Stroessner, whom Mengele had met several years earlier. Stroessner, like Argentine dictator Juan Perón, was sympathetic to expatriate Germans. Mengele decided he would be safer living permanently in Paraguay.

When Mengele returned to Buenos Aires, he ended his association with Fadro Farm, saying he had to leave the country for political reasons. He left his family in Argentina and, with the assistance of German war hero Hans Ulrich Rudel, obtained Paraguayan citizenship as José Mengele in late 1959. This pro-vided Mengele with extra protection against extradition to Germany, since Stroessner regarded Paraguayan citizenship as inviolate.

While living in Argentina, Mengele worked for his father's company selling Mengele farm equipment.

Israel Gets Involved

By this time the German government was not the only one involved in the search for Mengele. Israel's prime minister, David Ben-Gurion, directed Isser Harel, chief of the Mossad (Israel's intelligence organization), to hunt down war criminals who were still at large and bring them back to Israel to stand trial. Harel's two main targets were Mengele and former SS Lieutenant Colonel Adolf Eichmann.

Harel received word that Eichmann was living in Buenos Aires under the name Ricardo Klement and that his address was known. When he received a report indicating that another high-ranking Nazi official (supposedly Mengele) had been seen with him, he decided it was time to act. He traveled to Argentina to handle "Operation Eich-mann" himself.

Eichmann was located, identified, and kidnapped on his way home from work on May 11, 1960. He seemed resigned to his fate and spoke freely to his interrogators. He refused, however, to give them any information about Mengele. As Harel related in his book, *The House On Garibaldi Street*,

> He didn't disclaim acquaintance with Mengele, but he said he didn't know where he was and had never heard whether he was in Argentina or anywhere else in South America. Eichmann simply refused to say more, and to justify his refusal he told Kenet he didn't want to betray his friends. . . . When Kenet continued to press him, Eichmann brought up another argument in support of his refusal: he was afraid, he said, of what might happen to his [Mengele's] wife and children. . . . My impression was that he went into a panic when we demanded Mengele's location, and I felt that his obduracy [stubbornness] stemmed not from any sense of loyalty but from sheer fright.[48]

Another Move

Unknown to the Israelis and Germans, Mengele was no longer living in Argentina but rather in Paraguay. He was staying on a farm owned by Nazi Alban Krug near the Paraná River in southeast Paraguay, near the Argentine border. Eichmann's kidnapping sent him into a panic. Stories about Mengele's crimes began to appear in the German press, and the West Germans offered a 20,000-mark reward for his arrest. He came to the realization that he would never be able to return home to Germany, that he was destined to spend the rest of his life as a fugitive in South America.

By September 1960 Mengele's fear of capture by the Israelis caused him to move once again. Through Hans Rudel, he was put in contact with a fanatical Nazi—former Hitler Youth chief Wolfgang Gerhard—who was living in Brazil. Gerhard had been too young to play an important part during the war. He was thrilled to be given the opportunity to help protect one of the most notorious Nazis of all. Gerhard helped Mengele settle his affairs in Paraguay and placed him with Geza and Gitta Stammer, a couple looking for someone to manage a farm near Nova Europa, some two hundred miles northwest of São Paulo. Mengele was introduced to them as Peter Hochbichler, a former cattle breeder who had recently inherited some money that he wanted to invest in Brazilian real estate. He accepted the job for room and board but did not take a salary.

Although it became obvious that Mengele did not know much about farming (or care for the work, for that matter), the Stammers later insisted there was nothing suspicious about his behavior. He enjoyed giving orders

In 1960 SS officer Adolf Eichmann was taken into custody by Mossad in Argentina.

tower on the farm. When it was completed, he would spend hours in it, scouring the countryside for signs of activity that would indicate the presence of strangers who were looking for him.

Rumors and More Rumors

Despite all their efforts the Israelis were unable to locate Mengele. According to Harel, "By the end of the year [1961], we knew that he was moving between Paraguay and Brazil. He was completely panicked by the Eichmann abduction."[49] The Mossad kept Rudel under watch, waiting for him to make contact with his friend. They also tried to intercept mail sent to Martha Mengele, who was now living in Italy. All was for naught, however, as Mengele continued to elude his pursuers.

The West German hunt was also coming up empty. Rumors of sightings began to abound. Mengele was said to be protected by armed guards and watchdogs, to have an army of agents working for him, and to have killed an Israeli secret agent. Although none of these were ever proven, they added to the legend that was beginning to form around him.

to the farmhands and spent his free time reading and listening to classical music. He still feared capture by the Israelis, however, and began wearing a hat pulled down over his face at all times, no matter how hot the weather. He also supervised the construction of an eighteen-foot-tall wooden watch-

Mounting Tensions

Mengele remained with the Stammers for thirteen years. He depended on the couple for protection since he had never lived in South America on his own. With the money from his business ventures, he eventually bought an interest in their farm, as well as an apartment in a high-rise building in the industrial center of São Paulo as an investment.

Over the years, however, the relationship between Mengele and the Stammers had become strained. Not used to being told what to do by others, Mengele became more authoritative in the household. He tried to tell the couple how to spend their money, how to educate and discipline their children, and how to improve their marriage. He even forbade them to speak their native Hungarian in the house, fearing they might be plotting against him. "As time passed he even began to behave as if he was a superior human being," reported Gitta Stammer.[50]

In 1969 the Stammers moved into a new house in Caieiras, outside of São Paulo, so that Geza could be closer to his job. Mengele financed half of the purchase. By this time he had developed an interest in carpentry. He spent more time working on the house and less time arguing with the couple. It was not long, however, before friction between Mengele and the Stammers increased once again. Despite Gerhard's efforts to ease the mounting tension, it became obvious that Mengele would no longer be able to stay with the family.

The Bosserts

In an effort to ease tensions Gerhard decided to find someone else for Mengele to spend time with. The new friends he chose were an Austrian couple, Wolfram and Liselotte Bossert,

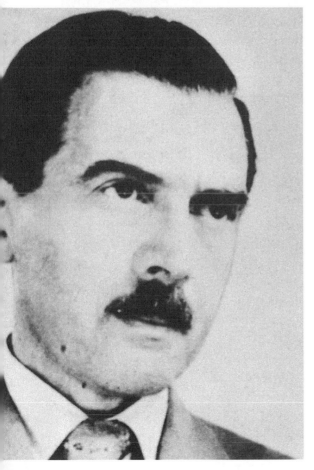

After Eichmann was taken into custody, Mengele, seen here in 1960, became very fearful of capture.

who also lived in Caieiras. Mengele—as Peter Hochbichler—got along well with the Bosserts, whose political leanings were similar to his. Former German army corporal Wolfram was also closer to Mengele's intellectual level than were the Stammers. The pair spent many hours discussing philosophy, music, and literature.

Through the Bosserts' efforts, Mengele began to emerge from his relatively isolated lifestyle. Said Wolfram,

> He was a man of complexes, frightened of leaving the house. When he went anywhere in a car he would hide his face with his hands. The result was that he actually drew attention to himself. He had that complex that everyone was looking at him. I told him that he was making himself conspicuous and I started to take him out in public more often, to the cinema, window shopping. It was a tremendous effort for him. He sweated with tension.[51]

The Bosserts finally convinced him to stop wearing his hat during the hottest days of summer. Eventually he started taking the bus and train by himself as he began to feel confident that the search for him had cooled off.

An Imaginative Account

One of the more interesting stories of a Mengele sighting in South America was told by former Brazilian policeman Erich Erdstein. According to Erdstein, he shot and killed the infamous doctor in September 1968.

Erdstein had convinced several newspapers that he was going to kidnap Mengele and hand him over to the Argentine police. In his book, *Inside the Fourth Reich*, he described how he laid a trap on the River Paraná. After grabbing Mengele, according to Erdstein, he and his son were on their way to meet an Argentine patrol boat when they were intercepted by a gunboat that began shooting at them. When six men from the gunboat attempted to take Mengele back, Erdstein opened fire and shot him twice in the back.

Certain Mengele was dead, Erdstein fled South America, telling authors Gerald L. Posner and John Ware, "After I killed Mengele, there was no way for me to stay. I wouldn't have lived long." He failed to mention a more likely reason for his departure: He was wanted by the Brazilian police for passing bad checks.

A New Identity

In 1971 Mengele was able to obtain a Brazilian identity card that had belonged to Wolfgang Gerhard. (Gerhard had decided to return to Austria.) With the help of amateur photographer Bossert, Mengele had his picture laminated onto the card over Gerhard's. Although the sixty-year-old Mengele looked much older than the forty-six years indicated on the identification card, Mengele felt safer with his new identity.

By this stage of his life Mengele was beginning to feel the effects of old age creeping up on him. Over the years he had developed a nervous habit of biting the ends of his bushy mustache. The hair that he swallowed formed what doctors call a bezoar and began to block his intestines. The condition became so painful that Mengele was forced to admit himself into a São Paulo hospital in July 1972 to undergo surgery. When the identity card raised questions about his age, Bossert told the doctor that the date of birth had been incorrectly entered and that a new card was being processed. Although the explanation was a bit far-fetched, the doctor believed him and accepted Mengele as Gerhard.

Mengele and Son

Faced with advancing old age and failing health (he was also suffering from an enlarged prostate gland and degeneration of disks in his lower spine), Mengele became acutely aware of the thousands of miles separating him from his family. He became depressed, knowing he could never return to his homeland. Mengele wrote many letters during this period of time, particularly to his son Rolf.

Rolf had been told his father's real identity in 1960 when he was sixteen years of age. Since then he had been plagued by questions about his father's actions during the war. To find out that the man whom he had thought of as a war hero was accused of having committed unspeakable crimes against humanity was extremely difficult for Rolf to deal with. "I had nothing in common with my father's views at all," he said. "On the contrary, my opinions were diametrically opposed.[52]

In his letters to his son Mengele always maintained his innocence of the crimes he was charged with at Auschwitz. Rolf was skeptical of the denials, despite their acceptance by other members of the family still living in Günzburg. He decided the only way he could resolve the matter was to confront his father in person.

Before any such meeting could be arranged, however, another problem had to be resolved. Mengele's friendship with the Bosserts had eased the tensions that existed between himself and the Stammers, but it was only a matter of putting off the inevitable. By early 1974 tensions had again reached the breaking point. The Stammers sold their farm in Caieiras and moved to São Paulo. They used part of the proceeds from the sale to buy a small bungalow, which they agreed to rent back to Mengele. He moved in in early 1975.

A Lonely Old Man

Living completely on his own for the first time since leaving Germany, Mengele's condition quickly worsened. He was plagued by a variety of physical ills, including high blood pressure, rheumatism, migraines, and insomnia. He lived a solitary existence, avoiding strangers as much as possible and sleeping with a gun beside his bed. Mengele still maintained some contact with the Bosserts and Stammers, but for the most part he led a cheerless life.

In May 1976 Mengele suffered a stroke that resulted in a two-week stay in the hospital. His false identity card again raised questions about him, but those who had any suspicions that he was a Nazi on the run either sympathized with his cause or were too afraid to say anything. Mengele's stroke did not result in any permanent paralysis but did increase the severity of his anxiety problems. His daily life became a constant stream of worries about his health, finances, and safety. The only thing that kept him going was the possibility of seeing his son.

Rolf's Visit

Arrangements for Rolf's secret trip to Brazil were finally made, and he arrived in mid-October 1977. The last time he had seen his father was in the Swiss Alps on Mengele's visit there as "Uncle Fritz" some twenty-one years before. In the intervening time, Rolf had learned that his father was accused of being a monster, arguably the most hated man on the face of the earth. Rolf's reason for making the trip was to confront his father and find out if what he had heard was indeed true. The pathetic old man who greeted Rolf when he stepped out of the Bosserts' rickety old Volkswagen bus, however, did not look like a monster. "The man who stood before me," he recalled, "was a broken man, a scared creature."[53]

Over the course of the next several days father and son spoke at length about the war years and Auschwitz. Mengele tried to justify what he had done, without saying exactly what it was that had transpired. He never admitted guilt, explaining that he had simply been carrying out his orders. Mengele tried to convince his son that his intentions had always been to help the people at the camp. "He said that he did not order and was not responsible for gassings," said Rolf. "And he said that twins in the camp owed their lives to him. He said that he personally had never harmed anyone in his life."[54]

After two weeks Rolf realized he was not going to get any more information out of his father. Mengele kept insisting that he only did what

The Boys from Brazil

Contributing to the interest in Mengele's whereabouts in South America was the 1976 publication of Ira Levin's novel, *The Boys from Brazil*. Two years later, the book was made into a movie starring Laurence Olivier, Gregory Peck, and James Mason. The movie is one of the first to seriously deal with the subject of cloning.

Olivier plays Ezra Liebermann, an aging Nazi hunter (patterned after Simon Wiesenthal) who receives a tip that Mengele (played by Peck) is alive in Paraguay. Mengele has ordered a group of assassins to kill 94 sixty-five-year-old civil servants around the world. When Liebermann researches the deaths, he finds that the men have identical adopted sons. Upon further investigation, he learns the boys are clones of Adolf Hitler, placed with their families by Mengele. In an attempt to recreate the events of Hitler's childhood, the men are to be killed since Hitler's civil servant father was also killed at the age of sixty-five. By having the clones raised under similar conditions, Mengele hopes to duplicate the *führer's* psychological makeup in his plot to launch a Fourth Reich. The movie sparked further attempts to locate the real Mengele.

Actor Gregory Peck played Mengele in the 1978 movie *The Boys from Brazil*.

Tourists line up to visit the house where Mengele lived in São Paulo. While living here, Mengele kept to himself and slept with a gun beside the bed.

anyone else would have done at Auschwitz in order to survive. He expressed anger and disbelief that his own son did not believe him. By this time Rolf knew there was no reason for him to stay. The visit ended with him leaving the São Paulo airport, certain that he would never see his father again.

The Beach at Bertioga

Mengele's physical condition deteriorated even more after Rolf went back home. In constant pain from his degenerating

Simon Wiesenthal, Nazi Hunter

The most famous Nazi hunter of all is Simon Wiesenthal. Born in Buczacz in what is now the Ukraine, Wiesenthal is a survivor of the Nazi death camps in which eighty-nine of his and his wife's relatives died. When World War II ended, he began gathering information concerning Nazi atrocities for the War Crimes Section of the United States Army. The evidence he gathered was used in the American zone war crimes trials.

Wiesenthal later helped establish the Jewish Historical Documentation Center in Linz, Austria, where information was gathered for use in future trials. When interest in prosecuting war criminals died down in the mid-1950s, the office closed. Wiesenthal, however, continued the work on his own. He eventually reopened the center in Vienna

and concentrated his efforts exclusively on tracking down war criminals. Wiesenthal conducts interviews, collects information, and presents his cases to the appropriate authorities whom he then tries to pressure into taking action.

Over the years Wiesenthal has won numerous medals and honors for his work. In November 1977 the Simon Wiesenthal Center was founded in Los Angeles. It is an international center for Holocaust remembrance, the defense of human rights, and the Jewish people. The Center carries on an ongoing fight against bigotry and anti-Semitism.

Death-camp survivor Simon Wiesenthal dedicated his life to bringing war criminals to justice.

spinal condition, he considered suicide. "Long-lasting pain of this kind causes one to be very nervous and sick of living," he wrote to a friend.[55]

Adding to his depression was the loss of a housemaid named Elsa Gulpian de Oliveira whom he had become very fond of. Although Elsa was almost forty years younger than Mengele, the two got along well, and he came to depend on her company. He told her he loved her but could not marry her. Mengele asked Elsa to move in with him, but she refused. When she told him in late 1978 that she was marrying another man, it dealt him a crushing blow.

In an effort to help shake Mengele out of his doldrums, the Bosserts invited him to their rented beach house at Bertioga Beach, a coastal community approximately forty miles north of São Paulo. He agreed to make the trip and arrived there on February 5, 1979. As he told his last maid, Inex Mehlich, "I'm going to the beach because my life is ending."[56]

On the afternoon of February 7, Mengele and the Bosserts left their cabin for a walk along the beach. With the hot sun beating down on him, Mengele decided to go for a swim in order to cool off. Within minutes Wolfram Bossert noticed the old man thrashing about in the waves. He swam out to his friend and dragged him back to shore. His rescue attempt, however, was in vain. Mengele had suffered another stroke while swimming. Efforts to resuscitate him were unsuccessful. The Angel of Death was dead at the age of sixty-seven.

Mengele was buried—as Wolfgang Gerhard—in Our Lady of the Rosary Cemetery on a hillside at Embu, twelve miles west of São Paulo. He was laid to rest in a family plot owned by the real Gerhard, who years before had arranged to reserve a grave next to his mother for what he said was an elderly relative. Mengele's family and friends did not reveal his death, believing it would raise questions about their roles in helping to hide him over the years.

CLOSURE

Mengele's death remained a secret for six years. During that time stories reporting sightings of the infamous Nazi doctor continued to appear in newspapers. A CBS *Sixty Minutes* program that aired in March 1979 presented evidence that Mengele had been living in Paraguay after Eichmann was kidnapped. Pressure was put on the Paraguayan government to arrest and extradite him, but Interior Minister Sabino Montanaro said Mengele had left the country years before, leading many to believe that he was dead.

Israeli Nazi hunters, however, were certain that Mengele was still alive. They argued that if he was in fact dead, his family would have reported it to the media in order to put an end to the unwelcome publicity and notoriety to which they were being subjected.

Rumors surfaced that he was living in Chile, Bolivia, Uruguay, and even New York. Speculation arose that he was involved in smuggling drugs into Miami. All such leads, however, resulted in dead ends.

The German government also believed Mengele was still alive. In 1981 the West German Prosecutor's Office drew up seventy-eight indictments against him. The indictments charged him with the following crimes:

Having actively and decisively taken part in selections in the prisoners' sick blocks, of such prisoners who through hunger, deprivations, exhaustion, sickness, disease, abuse or other reasons were unfit for work in the

Declaration of Amnesty

On the fiftieth anniversary of the liberation of Auschwitz, Mengele twin Eva Mozes Kor visited the site of the concentration camp and issued a remarkable Declaration of Amnesty. It read, in part,

I, Eva Mozes Kor, a twin who as a child survived Josef Mengele's experiments at Auschwitz fifty years ago, hereby give amnesty to all Nazis who participated directly or indirectly in the murder of my family and millions of others....

Look up to the skies, here in Auschwitz. The souls of millions of victims are with us—and I am saying, with them as witnesses: "Enough Is Enough. Fifty Years Is More than enough." I am healed inside, therefore it gives me no Joy to see any Nazi Criminal In Jail, nor do I want to see any harm come to Josef Mengele, the Mengele Family, or their business Corporations. I urge all Former Nazis to come forward and testify to their crimes they have committed without any fear of further persecution. Here in Auschwitz, I hope in some small way to send the world, a message of forgiveness, a message of peace, a message of hope, a message of healing.

NO MORE WARS, NO MORE EXPERIMENTS WITHOUT INFORMED CONSENT, NO MORE GAS CHAMBERS, NO MORE BOMBS, NO MORE HATRED, NO MORE KILLING, NO MORE AUSCHWITZES.

camp and whose speedy recovery was not envisaged.... Those selected were killed either through injections or firing squads or by painful suffocation to death through prussic acid in the gas chambers in order to make room in the camp for the "fit" prisoners, selected by him or other SS doctors.... The injections that killed were made with phenol, petrol, Evipal, chloroform, or air into the circulation, especially into the heart chamber, either with his own hands or he ordered the SS sanitary worker to do it while he watched.[57]

Auschwitz Survivors

By 1985, however, interest in finding Mengele began to cool. Even the Israelis were beginning to question the wisdom of continuing the search for a seventy-three-year-old Nazi. "After all," said Simon Wiesenthal, "when you bring an old man to court, there is a natural sympathy for him."[58]

On January 27, 1985, a group of inmate survivors gathered at Auschwitz to mark the fortieth anniversary of the camp's liberation by the Red Army. The event was reported by the news media around the world. A week later the survivors traveled to Jerusalem where a mock trial of Mengele was to be held. The purpose of the trial was to present evidence of his actions from the survivors of his experiments, in a final effort to bring the Mengele matter before the world.

The trial had its desired effect, bringing the group a flood of publicity. The day after it came to a close, U.S. Attorney General William French Smith instructed the Justice Department to open an investigation into Mengele's whereabouts. Soon afterward the Israeli government announced its own investigation. Countries and individuals from different parts of the world gave encouragement to the process by offering rewards for information leading to Mengele's capture. By the time they finished, he carried the largest bounty ever placed on a human being: $3.4 million.

In May 1985, representatives from the United States, Germany, and Israel agreed to share their intelligence and coordinate their efforts to find Mengele. One of the results of that agreement was a search warrant issued in Germany giving police the authority to examine the

Mengele died in 1979 at the age of sixty-seven, but his death remained a secret for six years.

house of Hans Sedlmeier, a childhood school friend of Mengele's and an executive in the Mengele company.

Over the years Sedlmeier had acted as a messenger for Mengele and his family, receiving and passing on letters between them. He had also channeled thousands of dollars from the family company to Mengele, enabling the doctor to live a comfortable lifestyle. During a thorough search of Sedlmeier's residence, the police turned up copies of letters that he thought had been destroyed but had actually been hidden away by his wife. "How could you do that?!" he exclaimed to her in disbelief. "Oh, my God, what an idiot!"[59]

The letters implied that Mengele was dead. Through them the police came up with the address of the Bosserts near São Paulo. From that point Romeu Tuma, the city's police chief, took over the investigation. He interrogated the Bosserts, who eventually told him that Mengele's remains could be found at Embu.

The Mystery Solved

On June 6, 1985, a horde of some two hundred people—including television cameramen, photographers, and police—gathered at the hillside cemetery at Embu. Three men dug at the grave site for an hour before their picks and shovels hit the coffin. Through the shattered lid could be seen shreds of clothing and weathered bones. The body did not have its arms crossed, as is the custom in Brazil. Rather, they were extended straight down by the side, in the manner in which Mengele had requested he be buried in letters found in Günzburg.

Dr. Jose Antonio de Mello, assistant director of the police forensic laboratory, reached in, removed the skull, and held it up for all to see. Noting the well-preserved state of the body, de Mello announced, "We should be able to identify the race, height, and color without much difficulty."[60]

Reports of the discovery of the bones were met with skepticism. Many people—including Simon Wiesenthal—were not convinced that the remains were those of Mengele. "Mengele lives and breathes," said Menachem Rusek, director of the Israeli police unit assigned the task of investigating Nazi crimes. "He and his relatives have already managed to play every sophisticated trick in the book to conceal his identity."[61]

Rolf Mengele, however, realized it was just a matter of time before the truth came out. "I have no doubt that the corpse exhumed at the cemetery in Embu is the remains of my father," he said. "I am sure that the forensic tests will confirm this shortly. . . . I have remained silent until now out of consideration for the people who were in contact with my father for the last 30 years."[62]

On June 21, 1985, a team of seventeen forensic specialists met at the São

Paulo federal police headquarters to reveal their findings. Having used modern forensic techniques—including a process known as "electronic supraposition" in which a microcomputer and television camera combined to superimpose photographs of Mengele upon the skull—they announced their conclusion.

Said Dr. Lowell Levine of the United States Justice Department, "The skeleton is that of Josef Mengele within a reasonable scientific certainty."[63] The forty-year search for the man who sent four hundred thousand people to their deaths at Auschwitz had come to an end.

NOTES

Introduction: The Personification of Evil

1. Quoted in Gerald Astor, *The "Last" Nazi*. New York: Donald I. Fine, 1985, p. 3.
2. Quoted in Pico Iyer, "Absolutely No Doubt," *Time*, July 1, 1985.
3. Quoted in John S. Lang, "Why the Nazi Hunters Keep Pressing On," *U.S. News & World Report*, June 24, 1985.
4. Quoted in Pico Iyer, "The Mengele Mystery," *Time*, June 24, 1985.

Chapter 1: Growing Up in Günzburg

5. Quoted in Gerald Astor, *The "Last" Nazi*, p. 13.
6. Quoted in Gerard L. Posner and John Ware, *Mengele: The Complete Story*. New York: Cooper Square Press, 2000, p. 5.
7. Lucette Matalon Lagnado and Sheila Cohn Dekel, *Children of the Flames*. New York: William Morrow, 1991, p. 40.
8. Quoted in Gerald Astor, *The "Last" Nazi*, p. 16.
9. Quoted in Posner and Ware, *Mengele: The Complete Story*, p. 8.

10. Quoted in The Jewish Virtual Library (www.us-israel.org/jsource/Holocaust/nurmlaw1.html).
11. Quoted in Gerald Astor, *The "Last" Nazi*, p. 25.

Chapter 2: Doctor Mengele

12. Quoted in Gerald Astor, *The "Last" Nazi*, p. 21.
13. Quoted in Gerald Astor, *The "Last" Nazi*, p. 22.
14. Quoted in The Jewish Virtual Library (www.us-israel.org/jsource/Holocaust/nurmlaw2.html).
15. Quoted in Astor, *The "Last" Nazi*, p. 23.
16. Quoted in Posner and Ware, *Mengele: The Complete Story*, p. 16.
17. Robert L. Koehl, *RKFDV: German Resettlement and Population Policy 1939–1945*. Cambridge: Harvard University Press, 1957, p. 64–65.
18. Quoted in Posner and Ware, *Mengele: The Complete Story*, p. 18.

Chapter 3: The Angel of Death

19. Rudolf Hoess, *Commandant of Auschwitz*. London: Pan Books, 1961, p. 126.

20. Quoted in Posner and Ware, *Mengele: The Complete Story*, p. 29.
21. Quoted in Wolfgang Sofsky, *The Order of Terror: The Concentration Camp.* Princeton, NJ: Princeton University Press, 1993, p. 206.
22. Hoess, *Commandant of Auschwitz*, p. 206.
23. William L. Shirer, *The Rise and Fall of the Third Reich.* New York: Simon and Schuster, 1960, p. 971.
24. Quoted in Flora Schreiber, "The Satanic Dr. Mengele," *The New York Times Syndication*, May 4, 1975.
25. Quoted in Michael Bar-Zohar, *The Avengers.* London: A. Baker, 1968, p. 234.
26. Quoted in Gisella Perl, *I Was a Doctor in Auschwitz.* New York: International Universities Press, 1948, p. 110-11.
27. Quoted in Posner and Ware, *Mengele: The Complete Story*, p. 46.
28. Quoted in Schreiber, "The Satanic Dr. Mengele."
29. Quoted in Astor, *The "Last" Nazi*, p. 89.
30. Quoted in Lagnado and Dekel, *Children of the Flames*, p. 80.
31. Quoted in Lagnado and Dekel, *Children of the Flames*, p. 81.

Chapter 4: Experiments in Terror

32. Quoted in Lagnado and Dekel, *Children of the Flames*, p. 46.

33. Quoted in Posner and Ware, *Mengele: The Complete Story*, p. 33.
34. Quoted in Posner and Ware, *Mengele: The Complete Story*, p. 31.
35. Quoted in Lagnado and Dekel, *Children of the Flames*, p. 47.
36. Quoted in Debbie Cohen, "Mengele Twin Tells of Selection, Survival," *Jewish Bulletin of Northern California*, April 19, 1996 (www.jewishsj.com/bk960419/sbtwin.htm).
37. Quoted in Posner and Ware, *Mengele: The Complete Story*, p. 34.
38. Quoted in Brian Ross, "Headaches for Bayer," *ABC News*, June 11, 2000 (abcnews.go.com/onair/2020/2020_990611bayer.html).
39. Quoted in Posner and Ware, *Mengele: The Complete Story*, p. 37.
40. Miklos Nyiszli, *Auschwitz, A Doctor's Eyewitness Account.* London: Granada Books, 1973, p. 53.
41. Quoted in Robert Jay Lifton, *The Nazi Doctors.* New York: Basic Books, 2000, p. 350–51.
42. Quoted in The Crime Library (www.crimelibrary.com/mengele/main.htm).
43. Quoted in Mark Weber, "Lessons of the Mengele Affair," *Journal of Historical Review*, vol. 6, no. 3, Fall 1985.

Chapter 5: Escape to South America

44. Quoted in Posner and Ware, *Mengele: The Complete Story*, p. 62.

45. Quoted in Posner and Ware, *Mengele: The Complete Story*, p. 71.
46. Quoted in Facts On File News Services (www.facts.com/icof/nurem.htm).
47. Quoted in Court TV (www.courttv.com/casefiles/nuremberg/hoess.html).

Chapter 6: Chasing Shadows

48. Isser Harel, *The House On Garibaldi Street*. London: Andre Deutsche, 1975, p. 219–21.
49. Quoted in Posner and Ware, *Mengele: The Complete Story*, p. 167.
50. Quoted in Posner and Ware, *Mengele: The Complete Story*, p. 222.
51. Quoted in Astor, *The "Last" Nazi*, p. 236.
52. Quoted in Posner and Ware, *Mengele: The Complete Story*, p. 234.
53. Quoted in Posner and Ware, *Mengele: The Complete Story*, p. 277.
54. Quoted in Posner and Ware, *Mengele: The Complete Story*, p. 279.
55. Quoted in Posner and Ware, *Mengele: The Complete Story*, p. 285.
56. Quoted in Astor, *The "Last" Nazi*, p. 246.

Epilogue: Closure

57. Quoted in The Crime Library (www.crimelibrary.com/mengele/main.htm).
58. Quoted in Posner and Ware, *Mengele: The Complete Story*, p. 304.
59. Quoted in Posner and Ware, *Mengele: The Complete Story*, p. 315.
60. Quoted in Posner and Ware, *Mengele: The Complete Story*, p. 319.
61. Quoted in Iyer, "The Mengele Mystery."
62. Quoted in Iyer, "The Mengele Mystery."
63. Quoted in Iyer, "Absolutely No Doubt."

FOR FURTHER READING

Books

Gene Church, *80629: A Mengele Experiment*. Richardson, TX: S.K. Damon, 1986. The true story of Jack Oran, who survived a series of bizarre experimental surgeries at Auschwitz.

Deborah Dwork and Robert Jan Van Pelt, *Auschwitz*. New York: W.W. Norton, 2002. The definitive history of the town and the concentration camp.

Deborah Dwork and Robert Jan Van Pelt, *Holocaust: A History*. New York: W.W. Norton, 2002. A new, exhaustive, insightful history of the Holocaust.

Eva Mozes Kor, *Echoes from Auschwitz: Dr. Mengele's Twins, the Story of Eva and Miriam Mozes*. Terre Haute, IN: C.A.N.D.L.E.S., 1995. A first-hand account of how twin sisters Eva and Miriam Mozes survived Auschwitz and Mengele's experiments.

Alan Levy, *Nazi Hunter: The Wiesenthal Files*. New York: Carrol & Graf, 2002. The biography of a man who has become a legend in his own lifetime, Nazi hunter Simon Wiesenthal.

Lore Shelley, ed. *Criminal Experiments on Human Beings in Auschwitz and War Research Laboratories: Twenty Women Prisoners' Accounts*. San Francisco: Edwin Mellen Press, 1992. A compilation of testimonies by twenty women who endured experimentation by the Nazis at Auschwitz.

Works Consulted

Books

Gerald Astor, *The "Last" Nazi*. New York: Donald I. Fine, 1985. An investigation into the life of SS physician Josef Mengele.

Michael Bar-Zohar, *The Avengers*. London: A. Baker, 1968. A look at the plans for Jewish vengeance against the Germans in the aftermath of World War II.

Erich Erdstein, *Inside the Fourth Reich*. St. Martin's Press, 1978. The story of a man who escaped Nazi persecution in Austria.

Isser Harel, *The House On Garibaldi Street*. London: Andre Deutsche, 1975. The riveting account of the capture of Nazi war criminal Adolf Eichmann by the Mossad.

Rudolf Hoess, *Commandant Auschwitz*. London: Pan Books, 1961. Self-portrait of the man in charge of the Auschwitz concentration camp.

Robert L. Koehl, *RKFDV: German Resettlement and Population Policy 1939–1945*. Cambridge: Harvard University Press, 1957. A history of the German program of resettlement in territories newly seized in World War II.

Lucette Matalon Lagnado and Sheila Cohn Dekel, *Children of the Flames*. New York: William Morrow, 1991. The stories of the twins who survived the notorious Auschwitz experiments of Dr. Josef Mengele.

Robert Jay Lifton, *The Nazi Doctors*. New York: Basic Books, 2000. A renowned psychiatrist examines the behavior and motivation of the Nazi doctors at Auschwitz-Birkenau.

Miklos Nyiszli, *Auschwitz, A Doctor's Eyewitness Account*. London: Granada Books, 1973. The memoirs of one of the physician-inmates of the infamous Nazi death camp.

Gisella Perl, *I Was a Doctor in Auschwitz*. New York: International Universities Press, 1948. A narration of the day-to-day events at the concentration camp by one of the physician-inmates.

Gerard L. Posner and John Ware, *Mengele: The Complete Story*. New York: Cooper Square Press, 2000. The definitive biography of the Angel of Death.

William L. Shirer, *The Rise and Fall of the Third Reich*. New York: Simon and Schuster, 1960. The complete story of the rise and fall of Hitler's empire.

Wolfgang Sofsky, *The Order of Terror: The Concentration Camp*. Princeton, NJ: Princeton University Press, 1993. A look at the concentration camp from the inside, as a laboratory of cruelty and a system of absolute power built on the businesslike extermination of human beings.

U.S. Department of Justice. Office of Special Investigations. *In the Matter of Josef Mengele: A Report to the Attorney General of the United States*. Washington, DC: U.S. Department of Justice - Criminal Division, 1992. (DD 247 .M46 U55 1991). Federal report on Mengele's whereabouts and postwar activities. Describes key findings of the investigation, including DNA test results on remains found in Brazil in 1985 and determined to be Mengele's.

Periodicals

Patricia Brennan, "Down to the Dirty Details at Wannsee, Approving Hitler's Secret 'Final Solution,'" *Washington Post*, May 13, 2001.

Pico Iyer, "Absolutely No Doubt," *Time*, July 1, 1985, p. 30(2).

Pico Iyer, "The Mengele Mystery," *Time*, June 24, 1985, p. 38(7).

Marguerite Johnson, "Hunting the 'Angel of Death,'" *Time*, May 20, 1985, p. 33.

John S. Lang, "Why the Nazi Hunters Keep Pressing On," *U.S. News & World Report*, June 24, 1985, p. 31(3).

Robert J. Lifton, "What Made This Man Mengele," *New York Times Magazine*, July 21, 1985.

Flora Schreiber, "The Satanic Dr. Mengele," *New York Times Syndication*, May 4, 1975.

Gavin Scott, "A Manhunt Leads to Bones," *Time*, June 17, 1985, p. 38(2).

Nancy L. Segal, "Holocaust Twins: Their Special Bond," *Psychology Today*, August 1985, p. 52(7).

"Visions of Hell," *Time*, February 18, 1985, p. 54.

Mark Weber, "Lessons of the Mengele Affair," *Journal of Historical Review*, vol. 6, no. 3, Fall 1985.

Internet Sources

Debbie Cohen, "Mengele Twin Tells of Selection, Survival," *Jewish Bulletin of Northern California*, April 19, 1996. www.jewishsj.com/bk960419/sbtwin.htm.

The Facilitator, "Politeness." http://209.87.142.42/y/f/f36.htm.

Brian Ross, "Headaches for Bayer," *ABC News*, June 11, 2000. abcnews.go.com/onair/2020/2020_990611bayer.html.

Websites

Court TV (www.courttv.com). Official site of the Court Television network. The Famous Cases section includes an account of the Nuremberg trials.

The Crime Library (www.crime library.com/mengele/main.htm). Part of the Court TV site, Crime Library is a rapidly growing collection of more than 500 nonfiction feature stories on major crimes, criminals, and trials. Joseph Mengele is listed under the Serial Killers section.

Facts On File News Services (www. facts.com). Official site of the Facts On File News Services. The Nuremberg trial is detailed in the Issues & Controversies On File section.

The Holocaust, Crimes, Heroes and Villains (www.auschwitz.dk). A site dedicated to the Holocaust, the systematic annihilation of 6 million Jews by Adolf Hitler and the Nazis during World War II.

The Jewish Virtual Library (www. us-israel.org). Official site of the American-Israeli Cooperative Enterprise's Jewish Virtual Library.

Max Planck Society (www.mpg.de/ english). Posts research in the natural sciences, life sciences, social sciences, and the humanities. Includes an apology on behalf of its predecessor, the Kaiser Wilhelm Society.

The Simon Wiesenthal Center (www. wiesenthal.com). Official site of the Simon Wiesenthal Center located in Los Angeles, California.

INDEX

PICTURE CREDITS

Cover photo: Hulton/Archive by Getty Images

AP/Wide World Photo, 43, 55, 61, 82

Archives of the Simon Wiesenthal Center, 26

© Bettmann/CORBIS, 20, 83, 87, 93

Central State Archive of Film, Photo and Phonographic Documents, courtesy of USHMM Photo Archives, 49

© CORBIS, 67

© Owen Franken/CORBIS, 80

Hulton/Archive by Getty Images, 11, 18, 21, 38, 41, 42, 73, 89

© Hulton Deutsch Collection/CORBIS, 33

KZ Gedenkstatte Dachau, courtesy of USHMM Photo Archives, 36

Library of Congress, 17, 23

Main Commission for the Investigation of Nazi War Crimes, courtesy of USHMM Photo Archives, 45

National Archives, 30, 68

National Archives, courtesy of USHMM Photo Archives, 46

Robert Nickelsberg/Time Life Pictures/Getty Images, 88

Brandy Noon, 13, 74

© Ira Nowinski/CORBIS, 63

John Phillips/Time Life Pictures/Getty Images, 77

© Michael St. Maur Sheil/CORBIS, 57

Yad Vashem Photo Archives, courtesy of USHMM Photo Archives, 52

About the
Author

John F. Grabowski is a native of Brooklyn, New York. He holds a bachelor's degree in psychology from City College of New York and a master's degree in educational psychology from Teacher's College, Columbia University. He has been a teacher for thirty-three years, as well as a freelance writer, specializing in the fields of sports, education, and comedy. His body of published work includes forty-five books; a nationally syndicated sports column; consultation on several math textbooks; articles for newspapers, magazines, and the programs of professional sports teams; and comedy material sold to Jay Leno, Joan Rivers, Yakov Smirnoff, and numerous other comics. He and his wife, Patricia, live in Staten Island with their daughter, Elizabeth.